254

W9-BJM-535

This study manual is written mainly to show you how to study the books of Numbers and Deuteronomy for yourself. Methods of Bible study taught in the earlier manuals of this self-study series (Genesis, Exodus and Leviticus) are used in this manual, with duplication of material kept at a minimum.

Introduction   Each lesson (except Lessons 1 and 10) consists of three parts: Analysis, Comments and Summary. Devote most of your time to the Analysis section, from which you will be led to various paths of your independent study. The Comments section is included mainly to interpret and apply selected portions of the passage being studied. The Summary section is brief and concise, intended to spotlight the prominent truths of the Bible chapters being studied. Whenever you begin a new lesson, refer back to the Summary section of the previous lesson for review.

As you study the Bible individually or in group discussion, continually ask those questions that will reveal more than surface facts. Counting on the Holy Spirit's help, be willing and anxious to dig deep for the matchless gems of Biblical truth.

You should always ask these questions concerning a passage:

What does it say?	(content)
Why does it say it that way?	(form)
Why is it located where it is?	(context)
What is implied?	(implication)

1

Seek to develop consistent and sound study habits, so that you can continually do more Bible study on your own. Never forget that the real purpose of Bible study is the spiritual fruit born by the Word in your heart. May your study of Numbers and Deuteronomy be that type of fruitful experience.

*   *   *

"Every scripture is God-breathed . . . ." (II Tim. 3:16, Wuest's translation)
"Holy men of God spake as they were moved by the Holy Ghost" (II Peter 1:21)

Publisher's Note

Enlarged charts related to the lessons of this study guide are available in *Jensen Bible Study Charts* (Vol. I, General Survey; Vol. II, Old Testament; Vol. III, New Testament). The charts are especially valuable for Bible study groups.

The 8½ × 11" charts can be reproduced as Xerox copies or as transparencies for overhead projectors. Selected transparencies are included in each volume.

NUMBERS
Background and Survey

USING CORRECT BIBLE STUDY PROCEDURE,

WE SHALL FIRST ACQUAINT OURSELVES WITH

THE BACKGROUND OF THE WRITING OF NUMBERS,

this fourth book of God's inspired writings; next we shall take a "skyscraper" view of the book; then we will be ready to analyze the individual parts. ("Image the whole; then execute the parts.")

I. BACKGROUND.

A. The Name.

Numbers derives its name from the two numberings or censuses of two different generations of the Israelites. The first was taken of the generation which left Sinai (chap. 1), and the second was taken of those who renewed the journey to Canaan (chap. 26). Other more appropriate titles, such as "In the Wilderness," have been given this book, but Numbers remains the standard title, having come down to the English Bible from early Greek and Latin versions.

B. The Author.

External and internal evidences point conclusively to Mosaic authorship of all five books of the Pentateuch, which includes Numbers. Moses certainly was the logical choice of God to record this story, since he was the chief eyewitness to the events.

C. The Date.

The events of Numbers followed those of Leviticus. The time span of the action of Leviticus was only one month, and Moses could have written that book before he left

3

Sinai for the next stage of the journey to Canaan. The time span of Numbers is almost thirty-nine years. (Cf. Num. 1:1; 33:38; Deut. 1:3.) Moses wrote Numbers when he was at Moab with his people, toward the end of his life at the close of the fifteenth century B.C.

D. Relation of Numbers to the Pentateuch.

The following study suggests interesting comparisons of the five books of the Pentateuch, as concerns some of their prominent teachings (other comparisons are made in this series' study books on Genesis, Exodus and Leviticus):

GENESIS	EXODUS	LEVITICUS	NUMBERS	DEUTERONOMY
Election	Redemption	Communion	Probation	Instruction
Promise	Pardon	Purity	Pilgrimage	Prospects

From what you know now of the contents of each book, show how the above words are representative of the books.

II. SURVEY.

There are three main stages of survey study: (1) making the initial acquaintance; (2) scanning the prominent individual items; and (3) searching for the integrating relationships. Keep in mind that the purpose of survey study is to see the book as a whole.

A. Stage one: Making initial acquaintance.

Read through the book of Numbers to get the feel and atmosphere of the book and to catch its major purposes. Write down your impressions of the book, and any key words and phrases that stand out.

B. Stage two: Scanning individual items.

1. Go through the book once again (a cursory reading is sufficient here) to secure segment or chapter titles; then record them on a horizontal chart. (Note: Refer to the survey chart, shown on p. 6, to obtain locations of segment divisions, but avoid studying the remainder of the chart at this time.) Remember that these titles are only

clue phrases as to content, and are not intended to serve as an organized outline.

2. Compare the first and last verses of Numbers, noting especially the geography. Refer to the map shown on page 8.

3. Recall what was said earlier in this lesson about the two censuses. Where do they appear in Numbers? _____

Why *two* numberings? _____

4. Read 10:11-13. Why does this begin a new section in the action of Numbers? _____
Chapters 13 and 14 might be considered the pivotal chapters of Numbers. In what way does the movement of the action of the book turn here? _____

_____

5. What was the "prize" God had offered the Israelites?

_____ In view of this, how appropriate is 10:29 as a key verse? _____

_____

6. Write out a list of the main persons and actions of Numbers which you recall as of your survey study thus far.

_____

_____

C. Stage three: Seeking integrating relationships.

Each book of the Bible may be studied as a single unit, with its many individual parts related to each other. In the survey study of a book we are trying to see how its various parts fit into the outline of the whole book. An important part of this study is to discover groupings of material of common content. Let us do that now for Numbers.

1. First, see how much you can do on your own before looking at the survey chart shown on page 6. The best place to begin is to look for the outline of geography in

NUMBERS   JOURNEY TO GOD'S REST-LAND

Two Key verses:
10:9 and 10:29

NUMBERED
PITCHED
TRIBE OF LEVI

	1 – 9	10:11 – 21:4	22:2 – 36
	AT SINAI	**TO MOAB**	**AT MOAB**
	PREPARATION for the JOURNEY	THE JOURNEY	AT THE GATE TO THE LAND
	INVENTORY AND ASSIGNMENTS	SINAI TO KADESH	NEW PROBLEMS
	PURGINGS, PRESENTATIONS, FINAL INSTRUCTIONS	DESERT WANDERINGS	FINAL PREPARATIONS
		KADESH TO MOAB	CONCLUDING TASKS
	— few weeks —	— about 39 years —	— few months —
	MT. SINAI	MT. HOR	MT. NEBO

Chapter/verse markers: 1, 2, 3, 4, 5, 6, 7, 8, 9, 10:11, 11, 12, 12:16, 14, 15, 16, 17, 18, 19, 20, 21:4, 22:2, 22:41, 23:13, 23:27, 24:10, 25, 26, 27, 28, 29, 30, 31, 32, 33, 33:50, 35, 36

Numbers. Then associate Israel's general experiences at these geographical areas, and you will have discovered the main thrust of the story of Numbers. Record your studies on your own survey chart.

2. Look for other related studies or outlines in the book, and record them. Make a comparative study of the significances of the three mounts: Mt. Sinai (chaps. 1-10); Mt. Hor (chap. 20); and Mt. Nebo (chap. 27).

3. Decide on a good title for Numbers, one that will accurately reveal the major theme of the book.

4. When you have finished your own original study, study the accompanying survey chart and compare it with your own findings.

Two important observations should be made here:

1. The Israelites in Moab at the close of the book, waiting to enter Canaan, are a later generation than the ones preparing for the journey at the opening of the book. This was because of God's judgment for the people's sin of unbelief and disobedience (chaps. 13-14).

2. Although the middle section of Numbers covers a span of about thirty-nine years, the text records very little of the events of these years of wanderings. They were literally years of waste and void, giving awesome testimony to the fact of divine judgment for sin.

* * *

Before leaving this lesson, we should alert our minds and hearts as to what areas of spiritual truth we may expect Numbers to emphasize. Here are a few of the more prominent:

1. Truths about God. Numbers has a lot to say about God—His grace, power, holiness, longsuffering, righteous judgments, and many other aspects.

2. Truths about God's people. Much is revealed of the weakness of the flesh: tendencies to murmur, doubt and forget the blessings of God, to mention only a few.

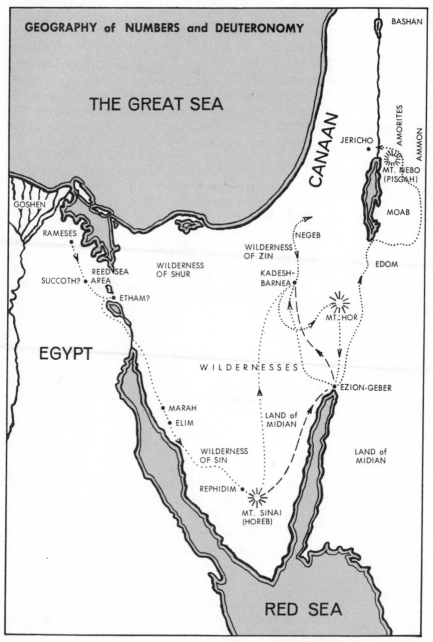

GEOGRAPHY of NUMBERS and DEUTERONOMY

THE GREAT SEA

BASHAN

CANAAN

AMORITES

JERICHO

AMMON

MT. NEBO
(PISGAH)

MOAB

GOSHEN

RAMESES

NEGEB

WILDERNESS
OF ZIN

EDOM

SUCCOTH?

REED SEA
AREA

WILDERNESS
OF SHUR

KADESH-
BARNEA

ETHAM?

MT. HOR

EGYPT

WILDERNESSES

EZION-GEBER

MARAH

ELIM

LAND of
MIDIAN

LAND of
MIDIAN

WILDERNESS
OF SIN

REPHIDIM

MT. SINAI
(HOREB)

RED SEA

— — — — — Alternate possible route from Sinai to Kadesh

8

3. Truths about the blessed everyday living that God wants His children to enjoy. To fully appreciate this spiritual lesson, read chapters 3 and 4 of Hebrews. The "rest" of these chapters is not heaven, but the normal, God-willed, Spirit-filled daily life of the Christian. Since Canaan is spoken of as that rest-land, we as Christians may learn much from the experiences of the Israelites on their journey to God's rest-land.

Inventory and Assignments

THE FIRST MAJOR GEOGRAPHICAL DIVISION

OF NUMBERS IS "AT SINAI," FOR THE ISRAELITES

WERE STILL THERE AS THE STORY BEGINS.

They had been encamped for a whole year. During that year they built the tabernacle and God instructed them about His will in a multitude of matters. He left them in doubt about nothing. He told them exactly how He would have them conduct themselves toward Himself and toward each other, even in minute details. The year of instruction was finished. It was God's will for them to march right up into the land and put all these precepts into practice. In this section (chaps. 1-10) He was getting them ready to move on.

On our survey chart we have called the section 1:1—10:10 PREPARATION FOR THE JOURNEY. Observe from the chart that only a few weeks were required to get this vast multitude of people in readiness for the journey. The important tasks of preparation were:

Inventory and assignments (1:1—4:49)

Purgings, presentations and final instructions (5:1—10:10).

Lessons 2 and 3 are devoted to these two sections, respectively.

I. ANALYSIS.

Read through the four chapters of this lesson in one sitting, observing the groupings of subjects, and underlining prominent words and phrases in your Bible for later reference.

1. What one thing about the instructions and procedures of these chapters strikes you as being prominent? _____

2. Chapter 1. What group among the Israelites was counted? _____

_____ The final tally? _____
From this, try to estimate the total population of all Israel.

_____ In view of such a vast multitude, what would normally be the problems of a march through a semiarid wilderness? _____

_____

Are miracles of God adequate for such problems? _____
Why were the Levites exempt from war? (vv. 47-53)

_____

3. Chapter 2. Record on a sheet of paper the positions allotted to the tribes and the tabernacle in the camp of Israel. (Note: The camp was spread over an area of many square miles.) Notice the references in the chapter to marching. What spiritual lessons may be learned from this chapter?

_____

_____

_____

4. Chapters 3 and 4. These chapters deal with the ministry of the tabernacle. Why is so much importance assigned to

the tabernacle? _____

_____ What was the relationship

of the Levites to the priests? (3:6, 9);_____

_____ to the Lord? (3:13) _____

_____ Do you suppose
there was any relationship between the Levites being chosen by God to serve the tabernacle and their earlier

response to Moses in connection with the golden calf (Exodus 32:25-29)? _____

(Note: You may have observed that the total census of the Levites is given at 3:39, 46 as 22,000, whereas the subtotals of vv. 22, 28 and 34 add up to 22,300. This may be accounted for by a scribal omission of one Hebrew letter in v. 28, reading 8,600 instead of the correct 8,300. Whatever the explanation, the 22,000 total is considered accurate.)

What was the difference between the two numberings of the Levites as found in chapters 3 and 4? _____

5. Can any spiritual lessons be learned from the fact of the numbering of a people, as found in these chapters? If so, what? _____

_____

Write out a list of ten other lessons taught by these chapters of Numbers. _____

_____

_____

_____

_____

_____

II. COMMENTS.

One is struck with the contrast between the book of Numbers and the book of Leviticus. In Leviticus the text is occupied primarily with worship, but the first thing that confronts us in Numbers is preparation for war. Today, we Christians also are engaged in battle. True, our wrestling is not against flesh and blood; but we have just as real and fierce a warfare on hand against the principalities, powers and rulers of this world's darkness. (See Eph. 6:10-18.)

Note on the chart the results of the census which Moses took at Sinai. Observe the relative strength of the tribes when they started on their journey—Judah the largest, Dan next, then Simeon, Zebulun, and so forth. At the end of the book a similar census was taken, and it is interesting to compare the two numberings in order to see which tribes increased and which tribes decreased during the thirty-eight years of wandering.

1. Reuben	46,500	7. Ephraim	40,500
2. Simeon	59,300	8. Manasseh	32,200
3. Gad	45,650	9. Benjamin	35,400
4. Judah	74,600	10. Dan	62,700
5. Issachar	54,400	11. Asher	41,500
6. Zebulun	57,400	12. Naphtali	53,400
		Total	603,550

The list shows the twelve tribes which were descended from the twelve sons of Jacob; but the names of two of Jacob's sons, Levi and Joseph, do not appear. In their place, however, appear the names of Joseph's two sons, Ephraim and Manasseh, whom Jacob adopted just before his death. (See Gen. 48:5-6.) Thus Joseph, the beloved son, is twice represented in the congregation.

Levi was not numbered among the warriors, because there was a special work appointed for that tribe (Num. 1:47-53). This was a great honor to be conferred upon the house of Levi. When Moses came down from the mountain and found the Israelites worshiping the golden calf, he called for those who were on the Lord's side to take their stand by him. All the sons of Levi gathered themselves to Moses; they would not soil their hands with calf worship. As a result their hands, and theirs alone, were appointed to touch God's sacred dwelling place.

In the second and third chapters we are shown the arrangement of the camp. The following diagram gives the probable arrangement of the camp. Notice that the tabernacle had the preeminent central position.

The Israelites were instructed not only on the order of encampment but also on the order of march. In both phases of their journey the tabernacle was to be central, for God was to be the center of all their living. They were never without this constant visible reminder along the journey.

Observe the assignments which the Levites were given concerning the tabernacle. The Gershonites had the care of such things as the curtains; the Kohathites, the furniture; and the Merarites, the boards (3:25-37). Each Levite knew exactly which piece of the tabernacle he was responsible

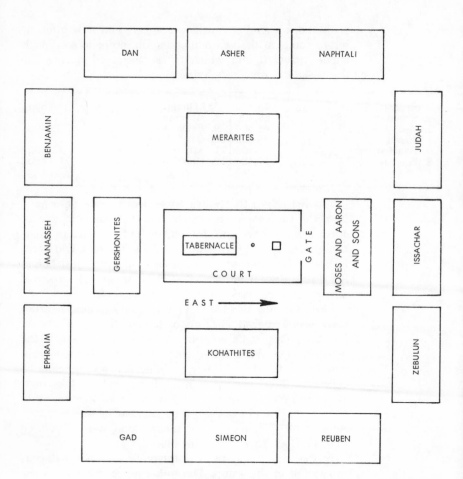

for. When the signal was given to move, each man took up his piece and moved on. Thus the tabernacle was quickly and easily moved without confusion or delay. Each had something to do. It was not left to a few to bear the whole burden. So today, each believer has been given his special place and work for God.

Each Levite understood that the part of the tabernacle assigned to his care was the work which the Lord had given him to do. A Levite, for example, could not abandon his work just because he might think that the bearing of the badger skins was unattractive or the carrying of the pins insignificant.

What work in the vineyard of God has been assigned to

you? Is it some obscure work which you sometimes consider monotonous or insignificant or unattractive? If God has given it to you to do, it is not insignificant; therefore, it should not be monotonous or unattractive. It has been wisely spoken, "Every one is not privileged to do magnificent things, but every one is privileged to do little things magnificently." Nothing is insignificant when done for the glory of God.

III. SUMMARY.

The order of business recorded by these chapters of Numbers concerned the major items of the Israelites' preparation for their sojourn to Canaan. First of all, there was the *organization for the journey,* which entailed:

1. Census of *warriors:* 603,550—for War

2. Assignments of *positions:* 12 tribes and the tabernacle—in Camp and on March.

Then, provision was made for the *care of the tabernacle* and its furniture:

1. Census of *workers:* 22,000 Levites (1 month upward)
8,580 Levites (30-50 years)

2. Assignments of *duties:* care and transport of the tabernacle.

Purgings, Presentations and Final Instructions

IN THE FIRST FOUR CHAPTERS OF NUMBERS

WE OBSERVED THE PREPARATIONS WHICH

ISRAEL'S CAMP AS A WHOLE NEEDED TO MAKE

before starting on the journey to Canaan. In this lesson we shall study the further preparations, especially as they involved individuals and smaller groups. Fix the following context outline in your mind:

PREPARATION FOR THE JOURNEY

CAMP AS A WHOLE	INDIVIDUALS
1:1 4:49	5:1 10:10

I. ANALYSIS.

First, read 5:1—10:10 in one sitting, looking not for details but for overall impressions and atmosphere. Among other things you may be struck by the large amount of space given to such repetitious content as that of chapter 7. Always keep in mind in Bible study that whatever is included in Scripture has a divine purpose, for "all scripture is given by inspiration of God" (II Tim. 3:16a).

In your second reading of these chapters you should begin to identify the various units of content, and then look for any groupings of these units. Try doing this first on your own, for most satisfaction in Bible study comes when you discover things by yourself. Record all your studies, using the horizontal chart method as a way of organizing your study.

Next, study the accompanying outline, comparing its divisions with those you have made. Be sure you understand why divisions are made where they are.

PURGINGS, PRESENTATIONS AND FINAL INSTRUCTIONS

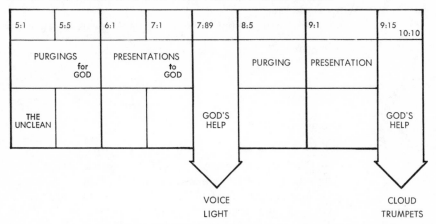

5:1	5:5	6:1	7:1	7:89	8:5	9:1	9:15 10:10
PURGINGS for GOD		PRESENTATIONS to GOD				PURGING	PRESENTATION	
THE UNCLEAN				GOD'S HELP				GOD'S HELP

VOICE
LIGHT

CLOUD
TRUMPETS

1. Observe the two sets of the twin theme: Purging—Presentation. Fill in the boxes with a title (one or two words each) that would best represent what the purging or presentation concerned. One example is given.

What is the intimate spiritual connection between purging (or cleansing) and presentation? _____

_____

Apply this to the Christian life.

2. Notice the two sections called God's Help. Show in what way the four words—voice, light, cloud, trumpets—speak

of that help. _____.

_____

_____

_____

17

_____ How significant is it
that these truths appear in these chapters of Numbers?

_____

_____

3. Continue your analysis of the individual sections of
these chapters by considering the following questions and
suggestions:
a. Read 5:1-4. What three ways of defilement are specified

in verse 2? _____

_____

_____ What aspect of sin

might be illustrated by each? _____

_____

b. Read 5:5-31. The main sin of this section is that of unfaithfulness regarding husband and wife. Read Hosea 1:1-9
for a striking account of God's views on unfaithfulness to
Him. Do you recall where in Israel's experience God said,
"I the LORD thy God am a jealous God"?
c. Read 6:1-27. The Nazarite vow was a voluntary vow of

separation. Separation from what? _____

_____ unto what? _____

Who of the Israelites could take the vow? _____

When, and how often? _____ What was the

primary reason for an Israelite to take such a vow? _____

_____

_____

Explain why verses 22-27 appear where they do. _____

_____ Relate them to what goes before,
and what follows. Who was the only perfect, heart-Nazarite

who ever walked the earth? _____

d. Read 7:1-88. What may have been the reason that God recorded at such length and with so much repetition, the gifts which the different tribes brought to Him? When were

these gifts presented? _____

Were the wagons and oxen practical gifts? _____

Were all the gifts practical? _____ What should be

the basic motive behind all gifts presented to God?_____

_____

e. Read 8:5-26. Why were there special cleansing ceremo-

nies for the Levites? _____

_____

What is the spiritual application? _____
f. Read 9:1-14. The main Passover is referred to in 9:1-5. Recall from your study of Leviticus the prominent place this commemoration had in Israel's experience. Verses 6-14 describe what is called the "little Passover." How do these

verses confirm the importance of the Passover? _____

_____

g. Read 9:15—10:10. Study the subjects of guidance and leadership here, and make present-day applications.
4. Complete your study by writing out a list of ten important truths in this passage which every Christian should know and practice today.

II. COMMENTS.

Numbers 5:1-4 clearly teaches how we must deal with sin. Not only must sin be put away from one's life, but discipline concerning it must be exercised by the church in certain instances. (Read Acts 5:11; Matt. 18:17; I Cor. 5; Rom. 16:17; II Thess. 3:6, 14; Titus 3:10-11; II John 10.) The reason for this great care about the purity of the assembly is given in the last clause of verse 3 of Numbers 5: "In the midst of which I dwell." The place where the holy God dwells must be holy. He will not dwell where evil or uncleanness is allowed or sanctioned.

Notice carefully the ordinance for the trial of jealousy described in Numbers 5:11-31. This was a positive command to be literally carried out by the Israelites. But it surely has a deep typical significance. In the Old Testament prophecies Jehovah Himself is spoken of as the Husband and Israel as the unfaithful wife. (See Isa. 54:5; Jer. 3:20.) Israel was unable to stand the searching trial, and was found guilty—proven to be untrue to her heavenly Husband Jehovah; and her unfaithfulness has been made manifest to the whole world. The application can be made to the church as well. Each individual believer should undergo thorough heart-searching, to see if there is any unfaithfulness to the heavenly Bridegroom, Christ. Sin is spiritual adultery.

The law of the Nazarite (Num. 6) is also instructive. Anyone could take the vow. It was a decision of utter devotion, to set oneself apart *to* God for a season, and therefore separate *from* certain things. Not that these things were sinful in themselves, but if indulged in they would interfere with this special consecration. No one *had* to be a Nazarite—it was perfectly voluntary; but if he did take the vow, there were certain things from which he must abstain. The Nazarite is a type of Christ, who from birth to death separated Himself entirely from everything that would hinder unbroken communion with the Father. Samson, Samuel, John the Baptist and others were said to be perpetual Nazarites, separated unto God from their birth, but Christ was the only perfect heart-Nazarite who ever walked the earth.

Numbers 7 should not be passed over hastily despite the repetitions of its verses. Each of the twelve tribes of Israel presented gifts to God, and exactly the same list of presents is recorded twelve times. God's ways are not as our ways even in writing a book—an uninspired human writer might have condensed this account into a few lines. Someone has observed, "There is no hasty promiscuous jumbling of names and offerings when God records the gifts of His children." He prizes even the smallest gift or slightest service, and carefully records all.

C. H. Mackintosh says: "This seventh chapter of Numbers is one of those specimen pages from the book of eternity on which the finger of God has engraved the names of His servants and the record of their work." The same writer adds that II Samuel 23 and Romans 16 are also similar chapters, where God records even the different shades of service rendered by His people; for example, "Salute Tryphena and Tryphosa, who labour in the Lord. Salute the beloved Persis, which laboured *much* in the Lord" (Rom. 16:12). If every believer has a page in God's book, with his name engraved at the top, and his gifts and services recorded thereon, how does your page look? Are entries recorded every day, or are there blank spaces of weeks and months when no offering has been brought to the Lord?

Another thing to be observed about this camp of Israel— this "church in the wilderness"—is that its movements were guided entirely by God's miraculous cloud which rested upon the tabernacle (9:15-23). Everything was done at the command of the Lord. Picture those two million people entirely dependent upon God for guidance as well as for sustenance. They were never sure how long they were to remain in one place, or where they were to go next. It was foolish to drive their tent stakes very deep or to become greatly attached to one spot, for at any moment they were likely to have to pack up and move on. They were to be looking upward constantly for guidance, to keep their eye on the cloud; when it moved, in whatever direction, they were to follow. What a beautiful picture of absolute surrender and dependence upon God!

Christians can learn much from this. All our movements should be controlled by God, and everything should be done at the command of the Lord. If the Israelites had attempted to go off on their own ways, or to stand still when the cloud moved, or to go forward when the cloud stood still, they would have hindered their progress toward Canaan. Similarly any attempt on our part to exercise our own will, go our own way or run before God, only hinders our progress in Christian living. We, too, should be constantly looking upward for guidance, following only where He leads.

III. SUMMARY.

In preparing for their long journey to Canaan, each Israelite family no doubt had many menial tasks (unrecorded in Numbers) to fulfill for their own well-being. These, however, were relatively minor and had no bearing on the success of the journey as a whole. The vital things were those which concerned *the place of God in the life of the nation,* and the preparations recorded in 5:1—10:10 relate to this. As you summarize this section of Numbers, observe the place of God in each part:

1. Purgings of the camp for God: the unclean, and the unfaithful.

2. Presentations of the people to God: Nazarite vow, and gifts.

3. The voice of God and the light of the tabernacle: for assurance of divine presence.

4. Purging of the Levites: for spiritual service.

5. Presentation of the Passover offering: for remembrance of deliverance.

6. The cloud and the trumpets: for guidance and leadership.

Sinai to Kadesh

THIS IS THE SECOND OF THE THREE MAJOR

DIVISIONS OF THE ACCOUNT OF NUMBERS,

WHICH HAS A VERY SIMPLE OUTLINE.

It is geographical as well as topical.

AT SINAI	TO MOAB	AT MOAB
1:1	10:11	22:2 36:13
PREPARATION for the JOURNEY	THE JOURNEY	AT the GATE to the LAND

The middle division is also divided into three parts, thus:

THE JOURNEY		
10:11	15:1	20:1
SINAI to KADESH	DESERT WANDERINGS	KADESH to MOAB

Our present lesson is devoted to the first part of the Israelites' journey as they moved from Sinai to Kadesh (10:11—14:45). Keep all of this context clearly in mind, for it will help in studying individual parts of the story.

23

I. ANALYSIS.

First, read through the section 10:11—14:45 in one sitting, observing such things as atmosphere, attitudes of the Israelites and the action of the story, including the words and actions of God and His appointed leaders. Observe and underline key words, phrases and verses. What are your impressions of the Israelites in the wilderness, after reading this account? What do you learn about human nature

from this? _____

_____

It would be profitable at this point to observe the geography of the Israelites' movements preceding these chapters. Refer to the map on page 8. Notice the dotted line of Egypt, across the Red Sea and down to Sinai. This marks the route taken by the Israelites under the leadership of Moses. They arrived at Sinai about three months after leaving Egypt (see Exodus 19:1); they remained at Sinai for about a year; and in Numbers 10:11-12 their journey is resumed. In Numbers 12:16 (see also Deut. 1:19 and Num. 13:26) they arrive at Kadesh Barnea near the southern border of the promised land. Note the dotted line from Sinai to Kadesh, and the alternate possible route via Eziongeber (marked by dashes).

Observe on the map the three great geographical areas: Egypt, The Wilderness, Canaan. They mark three distinct stages in the nation's history. In *Egypt* they were slaves of Pharaoh—downtrodden, poor, unhappy and groaning under their burdens. In the *Wilderness* they were freed from slavery and hardship and poverty, and were under the protection and care of Almighty God, who had made this His chosen representative nation. He was daily supplying their every need, but they were still unhappy, murmuring, complaining, dissatisfied, longing for Egypt and the things of Egypt. It was a new generation of Israelites that finally entered *Canaan,* God's promised land of milk and honey and rest from war (this story narrated by Joshua).

All this has deep symbolical significance. Those three stages of Israel's history suggest three stages of the soul's history. *Egypt* speaks of the condition of a soul before it is saved: a slave of Satan under bondage of sin and sinful habits. The *Wilderness* speaks of the unsurrendered Christian life. Though such a Christian has been freed from slavery to Satan and made a child of God, he is not fully surrendered to God's will. Consequently he is discontented, powerless and fruitless in Christian living. But *Canaan* speaks of the fully surrendered life of obedience which a Christian may live, wherein he is happy, contented, spiritually rich and victorious.

Come back to the text and analyze the smaller parts. Notice the outline with the five rectangles. Study each segment individually, with the outline in mind. (Each rectangle represents a segment, which is divided into paragraphs. Mark off the paragraph divisions in your Bible at the references shown in the rectangles.)

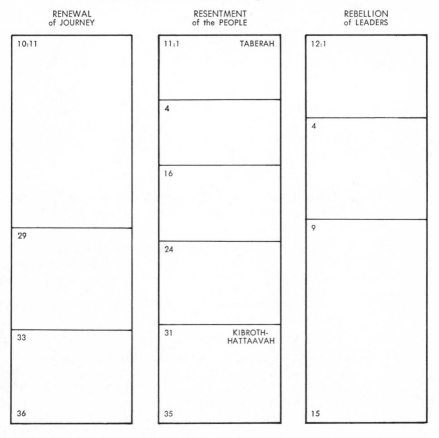

| RENEWAL of JOURNEY | RESENTMENT of the PEOPLE | REBELLION of LEADERS |

10:11 — 29 — 33 — 36

11:1 TABERAH — 4 — 16 — 24 — 31 KIBROTH-HATTAAVAH — 35

12:1 — 4 — 9 — 15

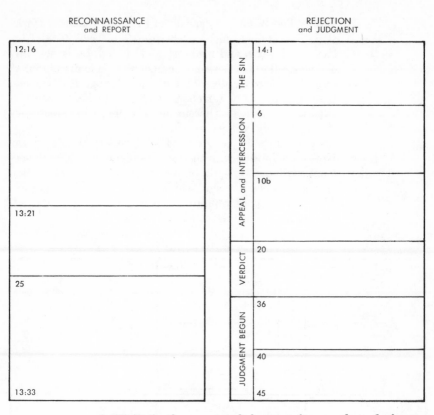

RECONNAISSANCE and REPORT

| 12:16 |
| 13:21 |
| 25 |
| 13:33 |

REJECTION and JUDGMENT

THE SIN	14:1
APPEAL and INTERCESSION	6
	10b
VERDICT	20
JUDGMENT BEGUN	36
	40
	45

1. Write in the paragraph boxes a few words and phrases that represent the key truths of each paragraph. Be as brief as possible without overlooking any major point.

2. Now look for relationships between paragraphs, as well as relationships between segments—such as cause, effect and sequel.

3. Here are some suggestions for the study of each of the segments:

a. Renewal of Journey, 10:11-36. How long ago had the census been taken? (cf. 1:2 and 10:11). _____
Write out in the paragraph box the order of march, including where in the order the bearers of the tabernacle and sanctuary were situated. Compare this order with that which the Israelites followed in camping. What was the

significance of the locations of the tabernacle and sanctuary furniture? _____

_____ What services did Moses seek from Hobab? (Note the word "how" of v. 31.) _____

_____ Read Judges 1:16 for whatever clue it gives as to whether Hobab agreed to be Moses' guide. Study verses 33-36 carefully, noting the importance of the ark, the cloud and Moses' prayers for Israel's journey. What spiritual lessons do you learn from this segment? _____

_____

_____

b. Resentment of the People, 11:1-35. After you have recorded key phrases in each paragraph, observe how these two subjects are developed in the segment:
  1) the people's complaint, and God's judgment (there are two sets of this sequence),
  2) Moses' burden, and God's help.
Show in the rectangle the locations of these situations. What was the difference between the people's complaints and Moses' burden (11:15)? _____

_____

Read verse 29 again. What did Moses mean by this? _____

_____ What are some important spiritual lessons to be learned from this chapter? _____

_____

_____

_____

c. Rebellion of Leaders, 12:1-15. Moses had problems not only with the multitudes, but with his own close associates. Proceed to study this segment as you have studied the others. Observe these two subjects and where they are recorded in the segment:

1) the leaders' envy, and God's judgment

2) Moses' innocence, and God's commendation.

Compare this segment with the previous one. From this passage alone what do you learn about Moses' character and ministry? _____

_____

_____

d. Reconnaissance and Report, 12:16—13:33. Chapters 13 and 14 constitute the pivotal section of Numbers, for the action in these chapters determines the destiny of the Israelites who began the journey with Moses. Study the commission given the spies regarding the people, land and cities of Canaan (13:18-20), and compare it with the report brought back (13:26-33). Account for the two commands spoken in this part of the commission: "Be ye of good courage, and bring of the fruit of the land" (13:20).

How did Caleb heed this charge? _____
List some vital spiritual lessons learned from this segment.

_____

_____

_____

e. Rejection and Judgment, 14:1-45. Record your observations in the paragraph boxes. Notice the outline shown. Be able to give the details of each item of the outline. What were the bases for Moses' pleas in verses 13-20? _____

_____

Why did God go through with the judgment already announced? (cf. vv. 12 and 23). _____

_____

Why was the people's confession of verse 40 not acceptable? _____

_____

II. COMMENTS.

In the first part of chapter 10 final preparations were made for the departure of Israel from Sinai. Moses was commanded to make two silver trumpets, which were to be used for calling the congregation together and as a signal for marching. When all things were ready, they got the order to start on the twentieth day of the second month of the second year.

Numbers indicates that when the Israelites were encamped the tabernacle was in the midst and when they were on the march the holy things of the tabernacle and sanctuary were still in the midst. Whether on the march or in camp, God had His people grouped around Him, as it were, in perfect order and harmony, each one under his own standard. Jehovah had come down "to dwell among them in their midst," and thus He kept His position. This should ever be God's position with His people. He should be the Center of church life, home life, individual life—the Center around which all things move and to which all things are referred.

From the time of the Israelites' encampment at Sinai until the time they departed (Num. 10), God's voice has been the prominent item in the Numbers account. But beginning with Numbers 11 we are again called upon to consider the people, and as usual it is very disappointing. Notice the opening words, "And . . . the people complained." It is not known why they were complaining. Under the circumstances they should have been joyous and thankful. Less than a year before they had been downtrodden slaves. Now they were a perfectly organized nation, having laws for their government which could not be improved. They were under the protection and leadership of Almighty God who made and upholds the universe. And they had the divine assurance that no people could stand before them and that they were marching toward a glorious land which would be their future home. Yet, instead of being filled with thoughts of these wonderful things, they were spending their time complaining about some little thing which did not suit their fancy. Why did they enter so little into God's great thoughts for them? They seemed unable to learn except by the most severe chastisement, and this time fire was the punishment which the Lord sent (v. 1). They ran to Moses like frightened children and he, towering in faith above them like a mountain peak, prayed for them; and the fire was quenched.

Next, the mixed multitude ("alien rabble," Berkeley version) caused trouble (v. 4). This mixed multitude which came up from Egypt with the children of Israel on the night of the Passover was a dangerous crowd to take along. People of mixed principles are dangerous in the camp of the Lord's people, and most congregations have some. They generally begin lusting for the things back in Egypt (the world), and they often lure the true children of God to their side.

The cause for the mixed multitude's complaint was their dislike for the manna food which God was supplying. They yearned for Egypt's fish, cucumbers, melons, leeks, onions and garlic. What a contrast to the food which awaited them in Canaan: pomegranates, grapes and figs and other delicious fruits.

When a Christian begins longing for things back in the world, he is inviting trouble. The fruit of the life typified by Egypt is described in Galatians 5:19-21. In contrast Galatians 5:22-23 describes the blessed fruit of Canaan, the Spirit-filled life of joy and victory.

To hear his own people murmuring again against God was a severe blow to Moses. He became thoroughly distressed. For the first time since Israel left Egypt, his strength and faith seemed to falter; then his words bordered on irritation against God. When he said, "Whence should I have flesh to give unto all this people?" (11:13) and "I am not able to bear all this people alone, because it is too heavy for me" (11:14), he seemed to have temporarily lost sight of God. Moses surely could not supply that vast company with flesh, but for Him who owns the cattle on a thousand hills, the Possessor of heaven and earth, it was no great task. Moses correctly observed that he was not able to bear all this people alone, but had God ever asked him to do so? Had not God promised from the first, "Surely I will be with thee"? No wonder Moses was discouraged; he had taken his eyes off God and saw only the people's demand and his own weakness.

Often God's servants stand in a place of heavy responsibility. But when they see the great need of the people and then lose sight of God, they will grow discouraged and cry, "Whence should I have food (spiritual food) to give unto all this people?" The source of supply is always the same in every time of need. Let us draw from this source continually.

God knew His faithful servant was a tired man, as was Elijah when he threw himself under the juniper tree and wanted to die. And as tenderly as the Lord dealt with Elijah, so He dealt with Moses. Instead of rebuking him, God lifted the burden and appointed seventy other men to help him bear it (11:16-17). Note how the Lord equipped them for service: He put the Spirit upon them and as a result "they prophesied and did not cease" (v. 25).

So God took care of Moses' burden. Then came the time for God to manifest His wrath over the people's persistent murmuring against His provision. The people were determined to have their own way, and nothing but flesh could satisfy them. So God caused a wind to bring up quail from the sea, all around the camp, in overabundance, to the extent of loathsomeness (11:31-33). The last phrase of verse 31 is correctly translated by the American Standard Version as "about two cubits above the face of the earth." The dead quails were not stacked two cubits (three feet) high *upon* the ground, but the live fowl were caused to fly that low *above* the ground, enabling the Israelites to gather them more easily.

Observe how eagerly the people gathered those quails (v. 32). They did not murmur about having to stand up "all day and all night and all the next day" to gather quails. But how would it have been if Moses had asked them to gather *manna* for that length of time? Some Christians do not seem to mind going all day and all night and all the next day in pursuit of some worldly pleasure; but if the Sunday services are prolonged a little past the usual time, or if the prayer meeting runs over the hour, loud and long murmurings are heard.

The Israelites kept eating quail for a month, until it became loathsome (cf. 11:19-20). But before they had devoured all the quail ("ere it ran short" is a better translation than "ere it was chewed"—v. 33), the "LORD smote the people with a very great plague" (11:33). The name given to that place was a fitting one, Kibroth-hattaavah, meaning "the graves of greediness." The people of Israel were given their own way, but many died as a result. Let us beware of stubbornly demanding that our will be done if our request is against God's will.

In chapter 12 trouble arises from an unexpected quarter: "And Miriam and Aaron spake against Moses." Aaron was the high priest, and Miriam held the highest position of any woman in the nation, being not only the sister of Moses and Aaron but also a prophetess. To think that these should rebel! The honors which God had placed upon them "went to their heads," and they could not bear that even Moses should be above them. With haughty hearts they cried that Moses was not the only prophet, for the Lord had spoken to them as well (v. 2). But God brought them out to the tabernacle and in very plain words told them it was not a question of prophets. Miriam and Aaron, to whom He spoke in a vision or dream, were indeed prophets; but Moses was God's faithful servant to whom He spoke intimately and to whom He manifested Himself. For her sin Miriam was struck with leprosy. She was healed only by Moses' prayers; but her rebellion delayed the whole camp of Israel seven days (v. 15). Why was not Aaron struck with leprosy also? Miriam, the elder, was probably the chief promoter in the rebellion, as verse 1 records her name before Aaron's, which is unusual when both a man and a woman are mentioned. Moreover, Aaron confessed his sin (v. 11).

The last verse of chapter 12 brings the children of Israel to the border of Canaan. Moses had fulfilled the promise made to them in the land of Egypt and had brought the nation up to the land which God promised to Abraham, Isaac and Jacob. We almost can see him as he stands before them, and says, "Ye are come unto the mountain of the Amorites, which the Lord our God doth give unto us. Behold, the Lord thy God hath set the land before thee: go up, and possess it" (Deut. 1:20-21). Moses probably never imagined there would be any delay in entering, no less any divine judgment prohibiting the people (and him!) from entering at all; he was to have the biggest disappointment of his life over this.

It took only ten men to persuade a nation of millions to defy the command of God to enter Canaan. These were the ten of the twelve spies who had been sent into Canaan to bring back a report on the fertility of the land; the character, number and strength of the inhabitants; and whether they dwelt in cities or tents. Up and down the land they went, surveying it forty days. Among the cities visited was Hebron, near where Abraham, Isaac and Jacob were buried. This place especially attracted Caleb, one of the spies, and he determined to get that part of the land for his own if possible. The spies took some of the fruit of the land—a great cluster of grapes, some pomegranates and figs—to show the people of Israel.

After the forty days' search, they returned to Kadesh to give their report. Imagine how eagerly they were greeted and how anxiously the people waited to hear what they had to say. The spies all testified that the land was just as God had said, a land flowing with milk and honey (Num. 13:27). If they had stopped just there, all might have been well; but ten of the spies went on to enumerate the discouraging things. Numbers devotes only one verse of three lines to record their description of all the beauties of the land, while four times as much space is used for what they told of the difficulties. As they proceeded with their recital (vv. 28-29, 31-33), the Israelites were beginning to shake with fear, and before the spies finished there was a regular panic among the people. In vain Caleb broke in (v. 30), and tried to speak. But the majority report triumphed, and the people began to weep and lament that they had ever started from Egypt or that they had not died on the way.

The spies had divorced God completely from their mind. They did not think of God. They did not see God. Not one mention of God was in their long speech. They were filled with unbelief, and the difficulties loomed before them like mountains, cutting off their vision. Unbelief always sees the difficulties. Faith always looks past the difficulties and sees God. Caleb and Joshua were filled with faith, and notice how differently they talked (Num. 14:7-9). Their speeches were not half as long as those of the other spies, but three different times they called attention to God. They too had seen all those high walls, great cities, and strong men, and did not at all ignore them; but far, far above all difficulties they saw their God, and they were depending not on their own strength, but on the Lord to bring them in (v. 8). The ten spies said: "We be not able to go up against the people." Caleb and Joshua did not deny this; it was perfectly true that Israel was not able to go against the Canaanites, but Caleb and Joshua said: "*He* will bring us into this land" (14:8).

The comparison was between "He" and "We." But the people would not heed these words of wisdom. They said the Lord had brought them out into the wilderness to kill them, and they wanted to appoint a leader and go back to Egypt. Imagine Moses' feelings when he heard them planning, before his very face, to appoint another leader. He might have reminded them of all they owed him—that more than once he had stood between them and God, and saved their lives by his intercession—but instead, as usual, he prayed for them.

Just at this critical time God again held out to Moses the offer He had made him once before (see 14:11-12). Again Moses stood like a rock, and contended for the glory of God and the good of the people, never giving a thought to himself (vv. 13-19). And again his intercession prevailed (v. 20). What a glorious character this Moses was—loyalty to God and self-abnegation were his chief traits. Did not God know Moses would stand the test? Yes. Then why ask him to endure it? Perhaps, among other reasons, so that the hidden grandeur of His servant's character might be revealed and recorded so that all the world might see and admire and imitate it—just as, it may be, God gave to Abraham the supreme test of his life largely for this same reason.

Observe that unbelief and disobedience kept the children of Israel out of Canaan at this time. They believed the spies instead of God. They would not believe God implicitly and obey Him absolutely. They were unwilling to surrender themselves to Him. This is just what keeps Christians from the Spirit-filled life. Absolute surrender to God in all things is necessary if one would enjoy victorious living today.

God told the people that because of their unbelief and disobedience they would wander forty years in the wilderness and be consumed, that not one of all those who had been numbered at Sinai as warriors, except Caleb and

Joshua, would enter the land (vv. 22-35). The people had declared that God had brought them out into the wilderness to die, so now God said that in the wilderness they should die: "According to your faith be it unto you." Caleb and Joshua said that God was able to bring them into the land, and God said: "Into the land ye shall come. According to your faith be it unto you."

With God's pronouncement, the people's doom was sure. But they hoped that God would still give them another chance, so they mourned greatly, made a rash confession of sin and began to march in the direction of Canaan. They were saying in effect, "We'll go up into Canaan after all." In all of this there was no contrition of heart, and they were presuming to spell out their own salvation. God was not with them, nor was the ark of the covenant, nor was their leader and intercessor, Moses. A host of them were smitten by the Amalekites. The judgment of God was beginning to take its toll.

III. SUMMARY.

The chapters you have just studied are the crucial chapters of Numbers. Recall the major movements of these chapters, writing out a few special items for each of the following segments of the outline:

Renewal of the journey

Resentment of the people

Rebellion of two leaders

Reconnaissance and report

Rejection and judgment

Desert Wanderings

THE ACTION-PACKED CHAPTERS STUDIED

IN LESSON 4 (SINAI TO KADESH) COVERED

ONLY ELEVEN DAYS OF ISRAEL'S EXPERIENCE.

The desert wanderings, the subject of this lesson, covered about thirty-seven years. (The duration of forty years is calculated to include the commencement and closing days of the wilderness experiences.)

When you read these five chapters you will observe that comparatively few events of the thirty-seven years are recorded. This is because Israel's existence during these years was merely one of aimless wandering; the nation was imprisoned within the walls of the wildernesses and was fulfilling the sentence imposed by God. If action is sparse in this section of Numbers, then the chapters are emphasizing some other important items. These shall be the object of your present study.

I. ANALYSIS.

1. First, read the five chapters without interruption. In this reading look especially for the *highlights* of the account, and the *general* content. Answer the following questions, referring to the text when necessary.

a. What two chapters are filled with action?_____

b. Considering the general content of the other chapters, why are these words spoken to the Israelites at this time?

_____

_____Are they directed to the generation dying off, or to the new one which would enter Canaan? _____

_____Cite verses to justify your answer. _____

c. What chapters concern special individuals or groups?

_____

_____What chapters relate generally to the whole congregation? _____

_____

d. Over what geographical area did the Israelites wander during this time? (Cf. 13:26; 14:25; 20:1; 33:19-36) _____

_____

Mark this wandering on the map on page 8.

e. According to God's sentence (14:29), how many people died during this period? _____

Figure out the average daily death toll. _____

_____Try to visualize the mammoth task of the Israelites in disposing of the corpses.

2. Now return to each chapter, analyzing the contents in more detail. Study the chapters in this order: 15, 19, 16, 17, 18 (reason for this order is given below).

Before analyzing chapter 15, observe the outline helps given in connection with the segment rectangles shown on accompanying chart.

Note: Chapters 15 and 19 have to do mainly with the entire congregation. One chapter concerns the commandments; the other, a special water solution of purification. Use the study hints given, to assist you in your analysis.

Write down key words and your own observations in the paragraph boxes and margins.

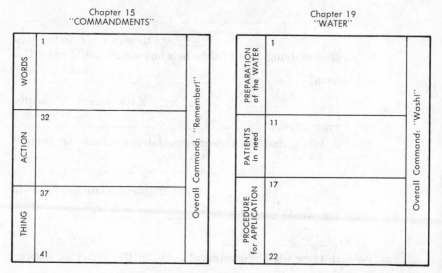

Chapter 15
"COMMANDMENTS"

WORDS — 1

ACTION — 32

THING — 37 ... 41

Overall Command: "Remember!"

Chapter 19
"WATER"

PREPARATION of the WATER — 1

PATIENTS in need — 11

PROCEDURE for APPLICATION — 17 ... 22

Overall Command: "Wash!"

Chapters 16-18 are about certain leaders of Israel. The three themes are opposition, vindication and provision. Look for these themes when you study each chapter. Record your own observations.

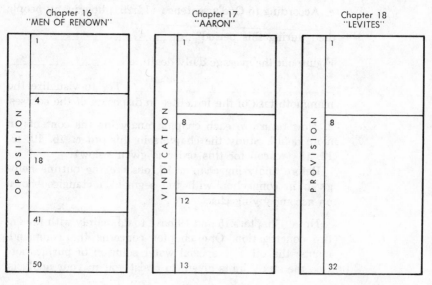

Chapter 16
"MEN OF RENOWN"

OPPOSITION — 1 ... 4 ... 18 ... 41 ... 50

Chapter 17
"AARON"

VINDICATION — 1 ... 8 ... 12 ... 13

Chapter 18
"LEVITES"

PROVISION — 1 ... 8 ... 32

3. Proceed further with your analysis of each of the chap-ters by following these study suggestions:

a. Chapter 15. Most of verses 1-31 is a restatement of com-mandments given earlier. Why the repeat?_____

_____What support does the second paragraph give to the first? _____

_____Observe the key word "remember" of the third paragraph. What does this para-graph reveal about human nature; about God?_____

b. Chapter 19. The defilement that is singled out here is that which comes from contact with a dead body. Why was this an especially pressing problem for the Israelites at this time? _____

_____Observe the various items of the first paragraph that had anything to do with the pro-duction of the holy water of purification (e.g., vv. 5-6).

What symbols of purification do you see here? _____

_____

c. Chapter 16. Were the leaders of the rebellion Levites or priests? _____ What was their alleged grievance? _____

_____

What was their real aim? (cf. v. 10). _____

_____Notice the way Moses gave honor to the service of the Levites (vv. 9-10). Apply lessons learned from this chapter to present-day problems of leadership in church work.

d. Chapter 17. How is this chapter related to chapter 16?

_____

Why did God desire to vindicate Aaron? _____

_____What was the ef-

fect of the rod's blossoming on the people?_____

How did God demonstrate once and for all that Christ was

His appointed High Priest? (cf. Heb. 4:14; 8:1) _____

e. Chapter 18. Notice the various references to gifts and
giving in this chapter. See how many different kinds of
gifts are cited. How should one look upon the opportunity

to serve God as a *gift* from Him?_____

_____

_____

4. Think back over the five chapters, and write out a list
of the prominent spiritual lessons you have learned.

II. COMMENTS.

Although the men who were numbered at Sinai were
doomed never to enter the land, their children were to enter and carry out God's plan. Thus the words of chapter
15 were for the benefit of these children, containing instructions regarding what they were to do "when ye be come into
the land of your habitation" (vv. 1-2). God, understanding
human nature, arranged that they should be constantly reminded of Him and His commandments. They were to put
a ribbon of blue (the color of heaven) on the borders of
their garments to keep them in such remembrance (15:
37-40).

In chapter 16 rebellion broke out in another quarter. It is
called the rebellion of Korah, because he was its religious
leader; but there were others belonging to the tribe of Reu-
ben who were associated with him (v. 1). These men gathered a number of the chief men of Israel around them
(v. 2), and took their stand against Moses and Aaron in the
words, "Ye take too much upon you, seeing all the congregation are holy, every one of them, and the LORD is among

them: wherefore then lift ye up yourselves above the congregation of the LORD?" (v. 3). They tried to make it appear that Moses and Aaron had usurped the position they occupied in the camp, and were thus interfering with the rights of the people. They also argued that since God was among them and all the people were holy, there was no need of a priest to serve as a mediator between God and men. Actually they were not after abolishing the offices; rather, they had their eye on replacing the officers. They despised those whom God had appointed—His anointed ones.

Moses wisely did not contend for himself in any way but was willing that the Lord should decide the whole matter. "And he spake unto Korah and to all his company, saying, Even to morrow the LORD will show who are his, and who is holy; and will cause him to come near unto him: even him whom he hath chosen will he cause to come near unto him" (v. 5).

Moses rebuked the rebels for not appreciating the honor that God had bestowed upon them. Further, he reminded them that they should have no feeling against Aaron, because the same God who had selected them for the service of the tabernacle had selected Aaron for his post (vv. 8-11). But these rebellious people would not listen to reason. They defied Moses' authority and taunted him for not bringing them into Canaan (vv. 12-14). The next morning, at Moses' command, they all stood before the Lord with their censers, and Aaron stood with his censer, to see whose worship the Lord would accept.

The question was decided in a way never to be forgotten. The earth opened and swallowed up the leaders (vv. 32-33), and the two hundred and fifty who had joined them were destroyed by fire (v. 35). The censers in which they had offered their incense were made into a covering of the altar, as a warning ever afterward that none but the seed of Aaron should offer incense before the Lord (vv. 39-40).

One would think that after such a terrible experience the people would be careful how they spoke against Moses and Aaron. But the lesson was not learned, for in verse 41 we read, "On the morrow all . . . the children of Israel murmured against Moses and against Aaron." They tempted the Lord to the point where all of them would have been consumed in a moment had it not been for Moses and Aaron, the very men against whom they were speaking. Read verses 47-48, and notice they were saved by *atonement* made by the high priest whom they had despised, and whom they had wanted to slay.

The plague was stayed by intercession and alert action, but not before fourteen thousand, seven hundred people died (v. 49).

God in His grace demonstrated to the people in yet another way that man must not defy His appointments of His own servants. Each tribe was instructed to bring a rod with its name upon it; and these rods—together with one bearing Aaron's name—were to be laid up in the tabernacle before the Lord. When they were brought forth the next day, they were all the same lifeless sticks as before, with the exception of Aaron's rod which had budded and blossomed and borne fruit. So the question as to whom God had appointed as high priest was settled by this miraculous sign of bringing life out of the dead stick—making the dead to live.

Was not the question as to whom God has appointed to be our High Priest settled by the same sign—making the dead to live? The resurrection of Christ proved Him to be what He claimed to be and assured us that His work (sacrifice) was accepted by the Father.

From this time on it was to be an undisputed fact for the Israelites, that only Aaron and his sons were to enter the tabernacle as priests. The people acknowledged that they could not approach the tabernacle and live. God answered their question, "Shall we be consumed with dying?" by the arrangement in chapter 18 that Aaron and his sons with him should "keep the charge of the sanctuary and the charge of the altar; that there be no wrath any more upon the children of Israel" (18:5). Thus the people were taught that they were to find their security in that very priesthood which they had despised and spoken against. At the same time God offset any tendency to conceit in Aaron by laying upon him the holy responsibilities as well as the privileges of the priesthood (chap. 18).

A careful reading of 18:20-32 reveals how finances were to be provided for the tabernacle service. The arrangement was as simple as it was wise. First, everyone was to give something, so that the burden did not fall heavily upon a few. When they reached Canaan, the land was to be divided and a portion given to each tribe, with the exception of the tribe of Levi. The Levites were to have no land but were to spend all their time working about the tabernacle. So God appointed that the twelve tribes (every man in each tribe) should give one-tenth of their yearly income to the Levites, and the Levites in turn should give one-tenth of this amount to the priests. These tithes, although used for the support of the priests and Levites, were counted by God as given unto Him.

According to chapter 19 God made provision for the purification of all uncleannesses, in the water of separation made of the ashes of a red heifer. By comparing Hebrews 9:11-14 we see that this sacrifice, like all the others, pointed to Christ. This ceremony showed the purifying effect of the ashes of the sin-offering when applied to man by water, and typified the purifying effect which the remembrance of our Sin-offering (Christ) has, when applied by the Spirit.

III. SUMMARY.

While wandering in the wildernesses, the new generation of Israelites who eventually would be allowed entrance into the promised land were given important instructions for Canaan living. They also learned more about the ministry of God's servants on their behalf. This may be summarized thus:

1. *The Israelites' Walk*
   —obedience to God's commandments (chap. 15)
   —cleansing of the heart (chap. 19)

2. *God's Workers*
   —chosen by Him, and so not to be challenged (chaps. 16-17)
   —provided for by Him through the gifts of the people (chap. 18)

Kadesh to Moab

AS OF VERSE ONE OF CHAPTER 20,

THE FORTY YEARS OF WANDERING

IN THE WILDERNESS WERE OVER.

The new generation of Israelites returned to Kadesh in the wilderness of Zin and prepared to move on to Canaan. (Cf. 14:32ff.; 20:1; and 33:38 for time references).

The story of these chapters is of two contrasting parts. The first part (20:1-29) tells of deaths and failures, while the second part (21:1—22:1) records successful marches and battles.

The map on page 8 shows the three general areas of the action of Numbers:

1. Mt. Sinai area (preparations for the journey)

2. Kadesh area (wilderness wanderings)

3. Moab plains area (waiting to enter Canaan)

Our study of this lesson follows the Israelites as they leave the second area and arrive at the third.

I. ANALYSIS.

Keeping in mind where you are in the book of Numbers, read these two chapters especially to catch the moods and atmospheres of the action, and to observe new and old things. Regarding the latter, what things that transpired here were similar to events recorded earlier in Numbers?

After you have acquainted yourself with the passage as a whole, analyze its two segments, recording observations on the accompanying charts.

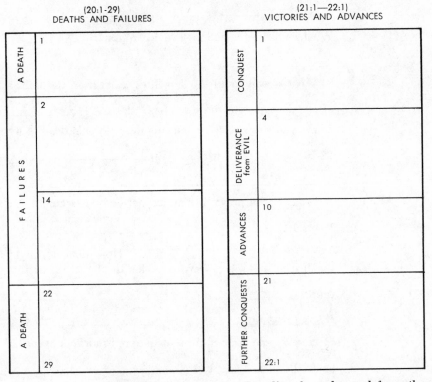

(20:1-29)
DEATHS AND FAILURES

A DEATH	1
FAILURES	2
	14
A DEATH	22
	29

(21:1—22:1)
VICTORIES AND ADVANCES

CONQUEST	1
DELIVERANCE from EVIL	4
ADVANCES	10
FURTHER CONQUESTS	21
	22:1

1. What lessons may the Israelites have learned from the deaths and failures of 20:1-29? _____

_____

2. The reference to Miriam's death is very brief. What strikes you about this, considering who Miriam was?

_____

3. What sin did Moses commit which kept him out of the promised land? _____

_____

In what way was Aaron partner in the sin? _____

4. Was God too severe in His punishment of Moses and Aaron? Justify your answer. _____

_____

What important lesson may we learn from this? _____

_____

5. What lesson could the Israelites learn from the failure of negotiation with the Edomites? (20:14-21). _____
6. Do you suppose the mourning over Aaron's death (20: 22-29) was of the heart? Explain. _____

_____

7. What is the prevailing atmosphere of the segment 21: 1—22:1? _____

_____How difficult might the test of endurance have been for the Israelites at this time? _____

_____

8. How do you account for the sin of murmuring appearing again (21:4-8)? _____
9. Read John 3:14-15. Show the ways in which the brazen-serpent episode symbolizes the truths of the gospel of Christ.

_____

10. How do you account for the new era of the Israelites' experiences—an era of journey advances and battle victories as recorded in Numbers? _____

_____

_____

11. Many spiritual lessons may be learned from these chapters. Write out a list of at least ten important ones.

II. COMMENTS.

Perhaps the saddest part of the Numbers story is the record of the sin of Moses and Aaron. Note carefully how the sin came about. The people were indulging in murmuring just like their fathers, this time because there was no water. It must have been more than a man as patient as Moses could endure to hear their taunts, sneers and regrets that they had ever left Egypt. However, Moses and Aaron went on their faces before God, and got explicit directions. Had these directions been carried out to the letter, all things would have been well. Moses was to take Aaron's rod "from before the LORD," where he had laid it up in the ark, hold it up before the people, and simply *speak* to the rock, and water would flow forth. It would seem that Moses understood these instructions perfectly. He followed them exactly (vv. 9-10) until he stood before the assembled multitude. But as he beheld the people and remembered how he had been blamed for everything that went wrong from the time Israel started from Egypt, he seemed to be carried away in a violent storm of anger and passion. Instead of speaking to the *rock,* he spoke rashly to the *people* (read Ps. 106:32-33); then he took the rod and smote the rock twice (v. 10).

For this sin Moses and Aaron (who was partner in the sin) were told that God could not use them to bring the people into Canaan (v. 12). Some think this was too severe a punishment for a slight offense. But it was not a slight offense. It was distinct disobedience and unbelief. Verse 12 gives the root of the whole matter. Moses and Aaron did not believe God with respect to this problem, and therefore did not obey Him. These sins of unbelief and disobedience were what had kept the old generation out of the land. If God had allowed Moses, who had committed the same kind of sin, to go into Canaan, He would have shown Himself to be a respecter of persons. But we observe also how tenderly God dealt with His servant. By letting the water gush forth, He honored Moses before the people, even though He had to take him away later and rebuke him in private.

Israel's high priest, Aaron, died at Mount Hor, after his priestly garments and duties had been transferred to his son Eleazar by Moses. One by one Moses' associates began dropping out of the ranks; soon he and Joshua and Caleb would be the only ones remaining of all the vast multitude that were numbered at Sinai.

After Aaron's death, God gave the Israelites victory in a battle against King Arad of the Negeb region just south of Canaan. One might call this a token battle, for it was an indication of the help which God would eventually give Joshua as he would lead the people into Canaan.

Then the people renewed their journey, having to take a longer route *around* the land of Edom, since they were not granted passage *through* it. The people grew discouraged, and as usual, began to speak against God and against Moses (21:4-5). As punishment for their discontent, God sent fiery serpents which bit and killed many of the people. When they confessed their sin and Moses prayed for them, God sent relief by the brazen serpent which Moses lifted up (v. 9). "And as Moses lifted up the serpent in the wilderness, even so must the Son of man be lifted up: that whosoever believeth in him should not perish, but have eternal life" (John 3:14-15).

Here is the gospel, preached in plainest language, by object lesson again. The Israelites had been bitten by the serpent and were dying. God lifted up the remedy which would give life to all that looked upon it. Just so, the old serpent, the Devil, has poisoned everyone of the human race with a venom of death. God has lifted up the remedy, Christ Jesus. All who look upon Him in faith shall live. But notice, each Israelite had to look for himself (vv. 8-9). Mothers then, as now, would probably have gladly looked in behalf of a serpent-bitten son who refused to look, but God's command was, "When *he* looketh upon it." Also notice, the dying one had to look at the lifted-up serpent, not at people, his own condition, priest or pole. "When he beheld the serpent of brass, he lived." Many today forfeit eternal life, because they are looking at something else besides the remedy which God has provided for sin-stricken humanity. They look at other people, at the church, at ordinances, but do not look to God's remedy, Jesus, in whom alone is salvation.

At this point in the experience of Israel their murmuring ceased. Evidently they at last learned their lesson and entered into something of the meaning of grace and gratitude; then they marched on in joyful victory to Jordan, conquering as they went. When their murmuring ceased, their singing began (21:17). This was their first singing since Exodus 15.

The Israelites moved northward, conquered the Amorites and dwelt in their cities (21:25, 31). Thus encouraged, they went on to Bashan (see map on page 8) until they conquered and possessed all the land of the Amorites east of the Jordan and "pitched in the plains of Moab on this side Jordan by Jericho" (22:1).

Thus their wilderness wanderings were over. They were just outside their promised inheritance, but much still had to transpire before they could enter and enjoy the land.

III. SUMMARY.

The story of these two chapters is the story of the renewal of Israel's journey to Canaan. The old generation had died off; the new could look forward to receiving the promised gift—the rich land of Canaan—from God. After some deaths and failures of God's chosen leaders, Israel overcame hindrances and enemies in its line of march, eventually arriving at the plains of Moab, opposite Jericho, to await entrance into the land.

New Problems

FROM THIS POINT ON, THE STORY OF

    NUMBERS CONCERNS THE ISRAELITES AT

    THE GATE TO THE LAND OF CANAAN.

By way of review, recall this broad outline of the book of Numbers:

JOURNEY TO GOD'S REST-LAND

1:1	10:11	22:2 36:13
PREPARATION for the JOURNEY	THE JOURNEY	at the GATE to the LAND

As indicated in the last lesson, there were new problems to be encountered before crossing the Jordan into Canaan, and these are described in the four chapters of the present study. The topics discussed in these last three lessons on Numbers are:

    Lesson 7: New Problems   (22:2—25:18)

    Lesson 8: Final Preparations   (chaps. 26-30)

    Lesson 9: Closing Tasks   (chaps. 31-36)

I. ANALYSIS.

1. Read 22:2—25:18 for your first impressions. Then read the following isolated passages, noting everything that is

said about Balak and Balaam: Numbers 31:8, 16; Deuteronomy 23:5-6; Joshua 13:22; 24:9-10; Nehemiah 13:2; Micah 6:5; II Peter 2:13-16; Jude 11; Revelation 2:14. You will notice from some of these verses that Balaam instigated the sins of chapter 25 though his name does not appear in that chapter.

2. The passage 22:2—24:25 is the story of a curse turned into a blessing. Among the things studied in this passage, observe and compare the words of Balak, the words of Balaam and the words of God.

3. An interesting study project is to find contrasts between the two segments of this passage. Look for contrasts in the areas suggested:

	22:2—24:25	25:1-18
	A CURSE TURNED into a BLESSING	A TEMPTATION LEADING to a PLAGUE
Passage in Numbers: long or short		
Opposition: internal or external		
Part played by Israelites in action of narrative		
Moabites' relationship to Israelites		
Effects on Israel of oracles and advice	Oracles of Balaam:	Advice of Balaam:
Hearts of Balaam and Phinehas	Balaam:	Phinehas:
God's view of Israel		
Outcome, as affecting Israel		

4. Make a list of some of the important spiritual lessons taught by these chapters of Numbers.

II. COMMENTS.

Let us reconstruct the story of Balak and Balaam in order to discover between the lines some of the motives and heart-thoughts of these men.

As the narrative begins, Israel is encamped in the plains of Moab, on the east side of the Jordan across from Jericho (Num. 22:1). This is in the vicinity of the territory occupied by the Moabites. (See map on p. 8.) Balak, the king of the Moabites, is thoroughly alarmed. He has seen how Israel has conquered the Amorites and possessed their cities, and his natural supposition would be that the Moabites and Midianites would receive similar treatment. As a measure of protection, Balak proposes to the Midianites that they send for Balaam to come and curse Israel. Midian consents, and the messengers depart. When they reach Balaam's home, they lay the case—and money!—before him. He bids them tarry all night, when he will inquire of God. God speaks to Balaam, telling him plainly: "Thou shalt not go with them; thou shalt not curse the people: for they are blessed" (22:12).

If Balaam's heart had been right with God, this would have settled the matter once for all. But it was not. In the morning he does not explain to the messengers *why* God will not permit him to curse the people, but simply says: "The LORD refuseth to give me leave to go with you" (v. 13). The messengers return to King Balak and simply make the statement, "Balaam refuseth to come with us" (v. 14), saying nothing about God. Balak evidently supposes he has not offered sufficient inducement to Balaam, so he sends again a larger and more honorable company. These are instructed to tell Balaam that he may set his own price and that, in addition, the king will promote him to very great honor if he will only come and curse the people (vv. 16-17). When this second company of messengers comes to Balaam, he tells them he is powerless to "go beyond the word of the LORD" (v. 18), but if they will tarry all night he will go again to God.

Balaam loves money, and Balak's gold and silver are proving to be tempting bait to this double-minded man. He hopes against hope that God will give him his own way. Balaam's heart is bent on going to Balak, and God lets him go; but He will not allow harm to come to Israel through Balaam's going. On the contrary, God will overrule it to their good. Balaam starts, and on the way the Lord meets him and tells him that his way (not his words) is perverse before Him (v. 32). Balaam says he is willing to return, but God is now going to use his mouth to bless rather than curse the people; so he is sent on with the men.

King Balak meets the prophet and the next day takes him up into the high places of Baal, from which point the white tents of the vast host of Israel can be seen stretching far into the distance. The Israelites are unaware at this time that an enemy king is trying to annihilate them. But their God is watching over them; and although Satan and all his hosts seek to curse them, He will not allow a breath to harm them.

Balak hopefully follows Balaam's directions, and erects seven altars, on which oxen and rams are offered. Then Balaam opens his mouth and lo—he is *blessing* the people! King Balak is astonished. The prophet whom he has brought to curse Israel is blessing them! Thinking that Balaam may have been frightened at the sight of the company of Israel, Balak takes him to a place where he can only see a part of the camp, and again offers sacrifices. But again Balaam blesses instead of curses the people. King Balak is greatly displeased, but he will try once more. He offers sacrifices the third time and Balaam blesses the people the third time. Now Balak is angry in dead earnest. He tells Balaam to flee, that he had intended to promote him to great honor but God had kept him back from that, and he must leave the country at once (24:10-11). Balaam leaves (24:25), but before he goes, he utters some prophecies against the surrounding nations. That is the story.

Balak tried hard to curse Israel, but God would not allow anyone to curse His people. Someone has aptly commented, "He may have to deal with them Himself in secret about many things, but He will not suffer another to move his tongue against them."

What was so wrong about Balaam? Look at other passages of Scripture which refer to him in order to know his character. From II Peter 2:15-16 we learn that Balaam "loved the wages of unrighteousness." Jude 11 tells us that Balaam was in error regarding this reward. From Numbers 25:1-3, in connection with Revelation 2:14 and Numbers 31:15-16, we gather that although Balaam had failed to get Balak's gold by cursing the people, he was determined to have it. So, back from his far-off northern home he came, and counseled Balak to cast a stumbling block before the children of Israel by inviting them to join in the worship of their gods, a worship that was accompanied by vile and obscene practices. Of course, if Israel would join the Moabites and Midianites in worship, there would be no need to fear hostilities. Such a peace plan delighted Balak. So the women of these heathen tribes beguiled the Israelites, and we read the sad result in Numbers 25:1-2 and 31:15-16. Balaam perished with the people who had hired him against Israel (Num. 31:8). Poor, wretched, self-willed, covetous Balaam! He said in one of his parables: "Let me die the death of the righteous" (23:10). Many others would like to die the death of the righteous; but they forget that the way to die the death of the righteous is to possess and exhibit the life of the righteous.

How did God speak through Balaam who was not an Israelite? Remember that although God had special dealings with Israel, He did not limit the revelation of Himself to that people.

The question is often asked, Do you think the ass really spoke? Why not? The Bible clearly says, "And the LORD opened the mouth of the ass, and she said unto Balaam . . ." (22:28). A. A. MacRae writes, "If Satan could enable a serpent to speak [as in Gen. 3], certainly God could make a donkey talk, if he chose to do so. It is not stated how God did this, but it is clear that Balaam heard an audible voice, coming from the animal."*

The marvelous prophecies uttered by Balaam show God's thoughts about Israel. Here a difficulty presents itself. From the words of these prophecies one might suppose there was no fault to be found with Israel. How could God say: "He hath not beheld iniquity in Jacob, neither

---

*New Bible Commentary, F. Davidson, A. M. Stibbs, and E. F. Kevan (eds.), (Grand Rapids: Wm. B. Eerdmans Publishing Co., 1953), p. 188.

hath He seen perverseness in Israel" (23:21), after all the iniquity and perverseness attributed to them thus far in the record of Numbers? We must remember that when God takes an individual or a people *to Himself,* He blots out their transgressions as a thick cloud. Though their sins be as scarlet He makes them white as snow; He casts their sins behind His back. God was looking at Israel as He looks at us, His children, today. He does not see us as we actually are in ourselves, but as what we are in Him.

See the progress of thought in these four prophecies. In the first one the main thought is separation. "The people shall dwell alone, and not be reckoned among the nations" (23:9). In the next one, the particular thing is God's presence: "The Lord his God is with him" (23:21). In the third prophecy, Israel is a channel of blessing to others: "He shall pour the water out of his buckets, and his seed shall be in many waters" (24:7); and in the fourth prophecy, we have a prediction of Christ: "There shall come a Star out of Jacob" (24:17). So in these four prophecies we see Israel as first, a separated people; second, a people among whom God dwelt; third, a people who are to be God's channel of blessing; and fourth, a people through whom the Deliverer of the race is to come. Moses was inspired to include these prophecies in the Torah no doubt as an incentive and encouragement to Israel concerning the nation's glorious future. We as Christians have a still more glorious outlook—one that should inspire us to heights of holy living every day!

As noted above, Balaam was not content to forfeit the prospect of material gain from the hands of Balak. Chapter 25 records the sad story of Israelite men being seduced by Moabitish women under the false pretense of religious worship.

Observe how the very nobility of Israel and Midian led in this shameless idolatry and impurity. The man who boldly brought a Midianitish woman into the camp, ignoring the weeping people before the tabernacle and the presence of the holy priests and their great leader, Moses, was not one of the common people, but "a prince of a chief house among the Simeonites" (v. 14); and the woman was a daughter of a chief house in Midian (v. 15). The wrath of Phinehas, the son of the high priest, was aroused at such outrageous disregard of holy things. Promptly pursuing the offenders, he slew them both. His zeal for God stayed the plague from the children of Israel (vv. 7-8); but 24,000 in all died at this time. God commanded that these Midianites be slain, and the execution of this command is recorded in chapter 31.

III. SUMMARY.

This lesson forcefully teaches the sovereign ways of God with reference to two of His main attributes: His love and His holiness. In love He graciously defended and blessed the nation whom He sovereignly chose (chaps. 22-24); and for His holiness His wrath was kindled against this same people, for their shameful idolatry (chap. 25).

Final Preparations

THESE CHAPTERS DESCRIBE SOME OF THE

FINAL PREPARATIONS ISRAEL HAD TO MAKE

IN ANTICIPATION OF CROSSING INTO CANAAN.

YOUR STUDY WILL FOCUS ON THESE THREE GENERAL SUBJECTS:

26:1	27:12	28:1 30:16
NEW COUNT	NEW LEADER	RENEWED OFFERINGS AND VOWS

I. ANALYSIS.

With the above outline in mind, read through the chapters. Record your impressions before proceeding further with your analysis of each part.

A. New Count (26:1—27:11).

1. What was the main reason for taking this census? (Read vv. 52-56.) _____

_____

2. Fill in the totals on the following tabulation. Then compare this second count with the first. How do you account for there being no increase in total population after forty years?

	First Numbering	Second Numbering		First Numbering	Second Numbering
1. Reuben	46,500		7. Ephraim	40,500	
2. Simeon	59,300		8. Manasseh	32,200	
3. Gad	45,650		9. Benjamin	34,400	
4. Judah	74,600		10. Dan	62,700	
5. Issachar	54,400		11. Asher	41,500	
6. Zebulun	57,400		12. Naphtali	53,400	
				603,550	

3. Why were the Levites not numbered among the children of Israel? (26:62). _____

_____

4. What was the request of the daughters of Zelophehad?

_____ Why did they make this request at this time? _____

_____ What was the principle behind the statute which God gave concerning this? _____

B. New Leader (27:12-23).

1. What does God identify as the *basic* sin of Moses? (vv. 12-14). _____

2. For more of the conversation between Moses and God (vv. 15-17), read Deuteronomy 3:23-27. What do you learn about Moses' character from these passages? _____

_____

3. What do you learn about Joshua in verses 18 to 23?

_____ How does he compare with Moses? _____

For certain counsel Joshua would have to consult the high priest, whereas Moses did not do so. What does this imply?

_____

C. Renewed Offerings and Vows (28:1—30:16).

1. Most of the instructions concerning the offerings described here already had been given at Sinai. Why were

they repeated here? _____

_____ What part would

offerings play in the life of Israel as they lived in Canaan?

_____ Recall from your

study of Leviticus some of the major purposes of offerings.

2. Record some observations about each of the following groups of offerings cited in this passage:

   a. Daily offerings (28:3-8).

   b. Sabbath offerings (28:9-10).

   c. Monthly offerings (28:11-15).

   d. Yearly offerings (28:16—29:40).

       1) Feast of Unleavened Bread (28:16-25).

       2) Feast of Weeks (28:26-31).

       3) Feast of Trumpets (29:1-6).

       4) Day of Atonement (29:7-11).

       5) Feast of Tabernacles (29:12-40).

3. Compose a list of some of the underlying aspects and intentions of these offerings as a whole. Think in terms of what God was trying to impress upon the hearts of the people through them.

4. What was the purpose of the regulations of women's

vows, described in chapter 30? _____
Keep in mind that the Israelites would soon be dwelling in a land of plenty. Who of the household was responsible

for the economy of the household? _____

II. COMMENTS.

It was almost forty years earlier that the adult males of Israel had been numbered at Sinai. Since then they had been falling by the wayside, sometimes one by one and sometimes in large numbers. "Their bleaching bones along the way tell the sad story of unbelief and disobedience." Probably the last remnant of those who started from Egypt and were numbered at Sinai had been swept away in the plague of 25:9. Those to be numbered were members of the new generation who either started from Egypt as children or were born in the wilderness. A large majority had never eaten anything but manna, and this was the generation which was to go over and conquer and possess Canaan.

Some interesting things can be observed about this second numbering. Compare the census which was taken at Sinai with that which was taken on the banks of the Jordan nearly forty years later.

First notice that after forty years there was a decrease rather than an increase in the total number. This in itself suggests something of the rigors of the wilderness journey. Contrast this with the phenomenal rapidity with which the Israelites increased in Egypt. The decrease well illustrates the unfruitfulness of wilderness life, that life which is out of God's plan. God's plan for Israel was for them to go directly to Canaan. If one is living an unsurrendered Christian life, of which the wilderness experience of this nation is a picture, he is out of God's plan for him, and decrease of power may be expected.

Judah, largest of the tribes in the first census, increased in size and retained its lead among the tribes. This is the tribe that was given the responsibility of leading the nation on the march and in war. This is fitting, because it was the tribe from which Christ came. But look at some of the other tribes. Simeon, for example, stood third in size, but in the second numbering it was the smallest. Numbers 25:14 may suggest an explanation of this alarming decrease. If many of the Simeonites followed the lead of their prince, many of them would have been among the slain.

Each of us should take spiritual inventories from time to time. How long has it been since you started from Egypt? How long since you were delivered from the bondage of Satan and began the new life with God? Have you increased or decreased in spiritual power? Are you stronger now to resist temptation than you were when you first became a Christian? Has your life touched the lives of unsaved ones, causing them to seek God and His kingdom? Does your life manifest the fruit of the Spirit—love, joy, peace, long-suffering, goodness, fidelity, self-control?

The major purpose of the census was to give Joshua a basis for an equitable assignment of the lands of Canaan to the various tribes. This is indicated in 26:52-56. The *size* of the territory allocated would be proportionate to the tribe's population (26:54), whereas the *location* of the territory would be determined by lot (26:55). One problem of inheritance that arose at this time concerned the disposition of a land deed when a landowner died leaving no son as an heir. Such a situation would not be uncommon in Canaan, and Moses was wise to see that the request of the daughters of Zelophehad was pertinent to the entire nation.

There was no law in Israel permitting women to inherit property, so there seemed no hope of these bereaved, helpless women getting a home in the promised land, now that they had reached its border. But they were descended from Joseph (v. 1) and, like their great ancestor, had strong faith in the goodness and justice of their God. So, ignoring all conventionality and precedent, they went to Moses and the priest, explained the case, and requested an inheritance. Moses immediately recognized that the matter needed divine legislation, for the disposition of *God's* land was involved. This was out of the jurisdiction of human counsel. "And Moses brought their cause before the LORD" (27:5). In the divine answer (27:6-11) the faith of these noble women was rewarded, and a law of inheritance was spelled out for succeeding generations, a law in force throughout the world even to the present day.

It must have been the most painful and difficult time of Moses' life to hear the Lord tell him to take a last look at the land he would never enter, and then to be told again that the reason for his being denied entrance was his rebellion against the Lord's commandments. But Moses did not begin to complain, nor to say he wished he had never started from Egypt, or that he wished he had died in the wilderness! See what did occupy his thoughts. "And Moses spake unto the LORD, saying, Let the LORD, the God of the spirits of all flesh, set a man over the congregation, which may go out before them, and which may go in before them, and which may lead them out, and which may bring them in; that the congregation of the LORD be not as sheep which have no shepherd" (vv. 15-17). God's work, and God's people, and God's glory, were first with Moses. And God fulfilled Moses' request and gave Israel a shepherd in the person of Moses' right-hand man, Joshua.

Chapters 28-30 of Numbers are often hastily and carelessly read, if read at all; but one of the most important lessons in the whole book can be learned from these three chapters. Here God is rehearsing the importance of the offerings and feasts as they were related to Him. Read the first two verses of chapter 28, emphasizing strongly the personal pronouns, and you have the lesson suggested. Then observe throughout these chapters the frequently recurring expression "unto the LORD." Underscore this expression in your Bibles in order to be reminded often of this important lesson. Very likely Israel had lapsed into a careless, formalistic performance of these offerings, with little regard for their significance, during the wilderness years. Before they entered Canaan God wanted them to realize their true character—that these services were not to be performed as a mere ceremony or formality, but every one was to be dedicated as "unto the LORD."

No doubt Israel needed to be reminded of this; but, surely, they could not need it more than we do in this present day. How prevalent is carelessness in the worship of God! Often the forms of worship are mechanical, with little thought of God. Frequently prayers are merely recited, hymns rendered and gifts collected, with no special thought of Him to whom all these should be offered. Let us apply the test personally and see if we need this reminder. Let us ask ourselves a few questions. When we start to church on Sunday mornings, what is the chief motive? Do we go because we are accustomed to or because we consider it respectable and right? Or is the uppermost thought in our minds that we are going "unto the LORD"? When we open our hymnals to sing, do we realize that we are singing these words "unto the LORD"? And if so, what is it we are saying? Do we mean the words, or are we singing carelessly, thoughtlessly? When we bow in prayer, do we feel we are actually addressing the great and holy God, Maker of heaven and earth, that the words we are repeating are being said "unto the LORD"? When the collection plate is passed, do we give simply from force of habit, or because we have promised, or with a view merely to maintain the expenses; or is it as though we were laying the money into the hand of Jesus, and offering our gift "unto the LORD"? "Whatsoever ye do, in word or in deed, do it heartily, as unto the Lord" (Col. 3:23).

III. SUMMARY.

The three sections of this part of Numbers are very appropriately represented by the simple words "unto," "over," and "unto," respectively. This is the key to the summary shown below:

NEW COUNT	NEW LEADER	RENEWED OFFERINGS and VOWS
INHERITANCE	MAN	OFFERINGS
unto the tribes	**over** the congregation	**unto** the Lord
"**unto** these shall the land be divided" 26:52	"Let the Lord . . . set a man **over** the congregation" 27:15	"These things shall ye do **unto** the Lord" 29:39

Concluding Tasks

IN THE LAST SIX CHAPTERS OF NUMBERS

MOSES AND THE ISRAELITES ARE ASSIGNED

LAST-MINUTE BUSINESS ON THE EVE OF CROSSING

into Canaan. (Numbers does not record the event of that crossing, nor does Deuteronomy, the last book of the Pentateuch. It is the purpose of these books to emphasize God's *promises* of the land and the *way* in which to inherit it. The book of Joshua records the conquest itself.)

Before analyzing the individual segments of this section, read through the six chapters at one time to get an overall view and the "feel" of the passage. Always keep a pencil in your hand as you read; use it to mark your Bible to show emphases and relations.

As an aid to orientation, the following simple outline should be kept in mind as you study. Observe that these concluding chapters present a perspective of Israel, as of the time of their waiting on the plains of Moab, in the three directions of present, past and future.

31:1		33:1	33:50 36:13
PRESENT		PAST	FUTURE
DISPOSAL of an ENEMY	DISPOSITION of a REQUEST	REHEARSAL of the JOURNEY	ANTICIPATION of CONQUEST

I. ANALYSIS.

A. Disposal of an Enemy (31:1-54).

1. Observe how *thoroughly* the Midianites were annihilated. For what sin was this judgment? _____

_____ How do you justify so *thorough* a judgment?

_____ Who received the spoils (goods) of war? _____

_____ How do you justify this, in view of the fact that Israelites had been guilty of sinning *with* the Midianites in the first place? _____

_____

_____

2. What may be learned about God, sin and judgment from this chapter? _____

_____

_____

_____

B. Disposition of a Request (32:1-42).

1. What did the Reubenites and Gadites want, and what were their real motives? _____

_____

2. Why did Moses at first refuse the request? _____

_____

3. On what conditions was the request granted? _____

_____ Even on the fulfillment of the conditions, would there always be a risk in connection with the arrangement allowed? If so, how? _____

_____

C. Rehearsal of the Journey (33:1-49).

Moses was commanded by the Lord to make a written record of the stopping places of Israel on their journey from Egypt to the plains of Moab. One reason for the record was to have it incorporated in the book of Numbers which God caused Moses to write. Very possibly Moses, on some occasion before his death, publicly read the journal before the princes and leaders of the tribes. If he did, what impact would such a rehearsal have made on their hearts and minds? To answer this question, read the chapter as though you were such an Israelite at that time, and see what truths impress themselves upon you.

The three geographical sections of this listing may be identified thus:

Egypt to Sinai:	33:1-15
Sinai to Kadesh:	33:16-36*
Kadesh to Moab:	33:37-49

At certain places in the listing Moses makes a special note of events that transpired at those places. Observe these instances, and try to explain the reason for Moses singling them out.

D. Anticipation of Conquest (33:50—36:13).

1. In the paragraph 33:50-56 is recorded God's commission to the Israelites in regard to the *degree* of conquest by which they were to enter Canaan. Observe how clearly God spelled out His mandate. How does this paragraph illustrate for the Christian today the requirements for entering into victorious Christian living—the "rest life" spoken of

in Hebrews 4? _____

_____

_____

2. The last three chapters concern items related to the allotments of the land. The four subjects treated are:

---

*The encampments of verses 19-36 are those of the thirty-seven years of wandering. These places are not mentioned in the earlier chapters of Numbers.

a. Outer boundaries of Canaan (34:1—36:13).

b. Levite cities (35:1-8).

c. Cities of refuge (35:9-34).

d. Preservation of tribal identity (36:1-13).

3. Note that the Levite cities were to be distributed throughout the land. What would be the advantage of this?

_____

_____

4. Why were there cities of refuge? _____

5. What was the purpose of the law, "Neither shall the inheritance remove from one tribe to another tribe" (36:9)?

_____

6. List some important spiritual lessons taught by these last six chapters of Numbers.

II. COMMENTS.

In chapter 31 the command which God gave in 25:16-17 is carried out. The exterminating of these Midianites who had beguiled Israel was the last matter of war with which Moses was occupied. This victory is remarkable; in fact, it is unparalleled in all history. Twelve thousand Israelites (v. 5) went against the innumerable hosts of the Midianites. Some idea of the numbers of the enemy can be gathered by noticing that after all the men and all the married women had been killed there still remained 32,000 virgin women (vv. 7, 17, 32-35). When the army of Israel was mustered to ascertain their own loss, they found that there was not a man missing (vv. 48-49). (Note: Not long after this, in the days of Joshua, there existed a nation of Midianites of large enough size to prevail against Israel seven years—Judges 6:1-6. Since the Midianites were of nomadic character, it is possible that those slain by Moses were of one group while their kinsmen, located at the time in some far-off place, were the Midianites who later vexed Joshua.)

Observe how the prey of conquest was divided (vv. 25-27). Half was to go to those who fought and half to the congregation who remained at home. Notice the tribute which was to be paid to the Lord. From those who went to the war one out of every five hundred was demanded as the Lord's, and from those who stayed at home one out of every fifty (vv. 28-31). Israel really should not have been involved in this war in the first place. If she had gone steadily on her way and resisted the wiles of the Midianites, the war would have been unnecessary. However, after she had conquered them, she was greatly enriched by the gold, silver, cattle and sheep which comprised part of the spoil. Is there anything for us to learn in all this? The Midianites represent the ensnaring, fascinating things of the world around us. The Christian should go steadily on his way, resisting all such allurements. If he yields to the influence of these things, he will suffer severe punishment, as did Israel. And yet, out of God's grace, if he repents and puts away such temptations in later situations, he can be strengthened and enriched by the very experiences which caused failure.

In chapter 32 a serious threat to Israel's success is recorded. The Reubenites and the Gadites had a great many cattle. Observing that the country which already had been conquered on the east side of Jordan was a good place for cattle raising, they came to Moses and requested that their inheritance be there and that they would not have to go over Jordan.

Moses was alarmed. He objected that this action on their part would tend to discourage their brethren. He reminded them how that nearly forty years earlier, when the people were at Kadesh-barnea on the border of the land, the spies discouraged them about entering, and God condemned the entire nation to wander and die in the wilderness. He warned them that if they now discouraged the people, God might pronounce the same judgment upon that generation. The two tribes then expressed their willingness to go over and assist in conquering the land, but desired that their families might remain where they were, and that after the conquest of Canaan was completed the men could return and settle down in their inheritance on the east of Jordan. Moses consented to this proposal, and gave instructions to Joshua and Eleazar to that effect. But Moses was very correct in objecting to a plan which would disjoin the nation geographically. History shows that an indifference toward the welfare of Israel on the part of the transjordan tribes eventually set in. The tribes caused great alarm to the whole of Israel, were much misunderstood and came to the verge of having war with their brethren, as seen from Joshua 22. In later years they were the very first to fall into the hands of the heathen enemy. In Genesis we studied about a man who chose his own dwelling place, because he considered it good for cattle raising, and we remember that he also got into trouble. God's choosing is always safest and best for us.

Chapter 33 gives a minute description of the wandering of the Israelites from the time they left Egypt until they reached Canaan. How touching to think that God's eye was upon His people in all their wanderings, noting their every movement. Not only that, He went before them every step of the way, providing for their need, bearing with their murmurings, patiently teaching them and caring for them with a divine tenderness! Surely there was never such a traveling companion. What God was to them, He is to us. He is with us all the way, and His eye is constantly upon us. Must He record as many haltings and turnings for our lives?

Many Christians are living in the wilderness verses of Numbers 33. They have no settled convictions, no fixed conclusions. It is characteristic of the wilderness life to "journey," and "remove" and "depart" from one opinion to another, from one position to another, "tossed about by every wind of doctrine."

See the important instructions given in verses 50 to 53. For these heathen inhabitants of Canaan the time had come when God would no longer bear with them and their abominations. You recall that during the time of Abraham they had been judged; but God had said, "The iniquity of the Amorites is not yet full" (Gen. 15), and had given them four hundred more years in which to turn from their wickedness. They had witnesses of God dwelling in their land—Abraham, Isaac, Jacob and Joseph—giving testimony to the true God. But these Canaanites did not like "to retain God in their knowledge," and so had gone from bad to worse until their condition was utterly corrupt, both morally and spiritually. Some faint notion of the depths to which these people had fallen can be seen by reading the fearful catalog of sins mentioned in Leviticus 18. They had become so evil that, as God expressed it, the land itself "vomiteth out her inhabitants" (Lev. 18:25).

Israel was to be God's instrument in driving these vile people out of the land, and they were to make a thorough work of it. They were to drive out all the inhabitants and destroy all their pictures, molten images and high places (Num. 33:52). Israel was to remove all trace of these people and everything that might remind them of these inhabitants in the future. This command was not only given as a judgment upon the Canaanites but also as a precaution against Israel becoming like them. Israel was so prone to turn from God that if any of the inhabitants were granted permanent residence in Canaan or if anything was left in the land to recall these evil ways, God's people would soon be swallowed up in the abominations of the land.

As it turned out, Israel did not obey God in driving out all the inhabitants of Canaan, as can be seen in Judges 1:19, 21, 27-35. In later years Israel found these unexterminated enemies to be "pricks in their eyes and thorns in their sides," just as the Lord had said (Num. 33:55). Furthermore, just as God had warned them (v. 56), He drove Israel out of the land as He had willed to do unto the Canaanites (Assyrian and Babylonian captivities).

Chapter 34 describes the boundaries of Israel's inheritance, "as drawn by the hand of Jehovah." If you take a good map and locate the identifiable places, you will see how extensive it is. The whole land was theirs, but they did not take possession of all. They possessed but a part of it, and that only for a time. How like ourselves! How little of our great inheritance in Christ do we actually possess! How little of the strength, wisdom, love and sweetness which is ours in Christ do we really have as our own!

Chapter 35 tells of the Cities of the Levites and the Cities of Refuge. The tribe of Levi was not to have a portion of the land like the other tribes. They were to minister constantly about the tabernacle. But they must have some dwelling place for their wives and children and the aged ones, so God graciously provided that the twelve tribes should give to the Levites certain cities, forty-eight in all, with suburbs for their cattle and gardens.

Out of these forty-eight cities, the Levites, in turn, were to give six cities, which were to be cities of refuge; that is, they were to be cities in which a manslayer (not a murderer) might find refuge from death. By God's command the murderers always were to be put to death. The law was very strict about this (see Num. 35:30-34). There was no opportunity for a murderer in Israel to buy his release (v. 31). But if a person *accidentally* killed another, he might flee for protection unto these cities which were named, well defined, publicly known and easily accessible. In Joshua 20 their names and locations are recorded. Some have considered these cities as a type of Christ, in that they were (1) of divine origin, (2) necessary to save from death, (3) accessible to all, (4) all-sufficient, (5) perfectly secure. There is one great contrast, however, that should not be overlooked: these cities received only the manslayer; Christ receives *all* guilty men.

*　*　*

SUMMARY OF NUMBERS

The book of Numbers very clearly illustrates the fundamental truths about the Christian's quest for happy, victorious day-to-day living in Christ.

The Israelites had good intentions when they left Sinai, but they failed the ultimate test of faith in God and obedience to His word. As a result, that generation of God's people forfeited the gift of the promised land and reaped the judgment of wasting the remainder of their years in the barren wilderness.

But there was a new day and a new start for a new generation, and these, together with the two who had not sinned—Joshua and Caleb—renewed the journey to the land.

Although Moses was not granted entrance to the land because of his sin, he nevertheless was used of God in a mighty way to serve and lead Israel almost up to the hour of crossing the Jordan. The following diagram may serve as a review of the highlights of Numbers:

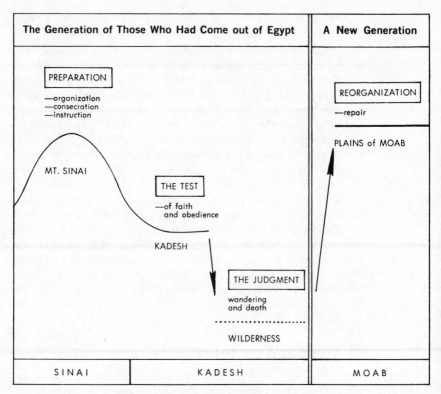

The Generation of Those Who Had Come out of Egypt		A New Generation

PREPARATION
—organization
—consecration
—instruction

REORGANIZATION
—repair

PLAINS of MOAB

MT. SINAI

THE TEST
—of faith
and obedience

KADESH

THE JUDGMENT
wandering
and death

WILDERNESS

SINAI	KADESH	MOAB

Just as the Israelites needed only to enter, by faith, into the land to enjoy its blessings, even so Christians today may enjoy the blessings of the indwelling Christ for living in like faith and obedience. "Let us therefore give diligence to enter into that rest, that no man fall after the same example of disobedience" (Heb. 4:11, ASV).

DEUTERONOMY
Background and Survey

ABOUT SIX HUNDRED YEARS BEFORE CHRIST,

JOSIAH, WHO REIGNED AFTER MANASSEH AND AMON,

COMMANDED THAT THE HOUSE OF THE LORD

be repaired and cleansed of all the abominations which Manasseh had brought in (II Kings 22). In clearing out the temple, the workers found the book of the law which had lain unnoticed and unread for many years (cf. Deut. 31:24-26). When it was read before the king and the people, great was their horror and consternation on hearing God's denunciations against idolatry. They realized that idolatry already was fully established in the land and that there was no escape from the judgment which God had pronounced so long before on this sin.

Hundreds of years earlier Moses had written the "words of the book of the law" and most emphatically commanded that the book should be kept constantly before the people. They were told to read and study it every day, to obey it and teach it to their children and to talk of it continually (see Deut. 6:6-9). Especially were the *kings* commanded to read and observe the teachings of the book (Deut. 17:18-20). If God's people had followed these instructions they would not have fallen so far away from Him. But they neglected the precious book containing their Lord's commands, as too many of God's children neglect their Bible today. Therefore, it is no wonder they were led into the idolatrous ways of the heathen. This episode in Israel's history should serve as solemn warning to Christians to not neglect the daily reading and the obeying of God's holy Word. The whole church needs to be aroused concerning this. All the sin, worldliness, heresy and error which have ever plagued the church have resulted from the neglect of God's Word—either neglect to know it or neglect to obey it.

Thus it readily can be seen how important a study of Deuteronomy is for Christians today. Our study of this book will be more brief than that of Numbers, but we cannot afford to overlook any of the more prominent truths taught by a book that played such a vital role in Israel's history. First we shall look at the background of this fifth and final part of the law; then we shall make a preliminary survey of the book as a whole.

I. BACKGROUND.

A. Title and Position in the Pentateuch.

Our English title *Deuteronomy* is traced back to the Greek Septuagint version of the Old Testament where the title was given as *Deuteronomion,* meaning literally "second law-giving" or "law repeated." This title obviously referred to the fact that the book was a restatement of the laws which already had been given by God through Moses, as recorded in Exodus, Leviticus and Numbers. The title which the Jews have assigned to this book is *Debarim* ("Words"), a title derived, according to their custom, from the opening line of 1:1.

Within the group of the Pentateuch books, Deuteronomy resembles Leviticus in its paucity of action sections. The books are also similar in that the instructions contained in each were given to Israel while they were in standby encampment at Sinai and on the plains of Moab. In Leviticus they were anticipating their wandering life, and in Deuteronomy they were making preparations for their settled life in Canaan. The two books are different in that Leviticus was given mainly for the instruction of the priests and Levites while Deuteronomy was given to instruct the common man.

Deuteronomy has been called the Book of Review. But it was given for more than just a review of Israel's past—it also looked into the future. Someone, in comparing the five books of Moses, has written this:

> In Genesis God selects a field in which to sow the seed of His law; that field of course is the Israelitish nation. In Exodus He purchases and secures the field. In Leviticus He brings forth His seed but finds the ground hard and thorny. In Numbers, for forty years He is plowing, clearing and preparing the field; in Deuteronomy He is again sowing the seed and harrowing it in.

Surely Moses, as he patiently rehearses God's law in Deuteronomy and over and over again repeats his injunction to "hear" and "keep" and "do," might well be said to be harrowing the law of God into the minds and hearts of the people, that they might succeed and live victoriously in Canaan.

Deuteronomy also supplements, by additions or explanations, some of the things already recorded in the earlier books. For example, in Numbers we are told that elders were appointed to assist Moses, but the instructions which Moses gave these judges at that time are recorded in Deuteronomy (1:16-17). Also, in Numbers we are told that the spies were sent from Kadesh-barnea, but not until Deuteronomy 1:19-23 do we hear of the request originating with the people. Further, in Numbers Moses was forbidden to enter Canaan, but the conversation between him and God was not recorded until Deuteronomy 3:23-26.

B. Author.

Evidence for Mosaic authorship is overwhelming. At places in the text he is expressly identified as the author (read 1:1-6; 4:44-46; 29:1; 31:9, 24-26). Jewish and Samaritan tradition has assigned the book to Moses. Jesus and New Testament writers, who quote from Deuteronomy more than from any other Old Testament book (about eighty times; read Rom. 10:6-8; Heb. 12:29; 13:5; Matt. 4:4, 7, 10; 22:37-38), associate the book with the law. Internally, its message best fits the times and ministry of Moses. "The words are instinct with the warm solicitude of a great leader for the people whose experiences he had shared."*

Of course chapter 34, which records Moses' death, was written by another person. Of this Gleason Archer writes, "The closing chapter furnishes only that type of obituary which is often appended to the final work of great men of letters . . . ."† Joshua, Moses' friend and successor, may have written the obituary.

C. Setting.

The circumstances under which Deuteronomy was written are clear. Israel had reached the border of Canaan. Forty years earlier the nation had been on the border of the land, but because of unbelief and disobedience the people were not allowed to enter. This time they had to tarry on the banks of the Jordan until they learned this one lesson: "They must obey their God." God was willing and ready to lead them on to victory and to give them the delights of the land, but this was absolutely impossible until they would bend their stubborn wills and surrender entirely to God. Moses, the lawgiver, was about to leave them; so he gathered his beloved people around him for the last time and delivered his farewell address—Deuteronomy. His object in the address, and hence the object of the book, was to impress upon them the one lesson: obey, obey, obey.

II. SURVEY.

A. Survey Reading.

You are already acquainted with the purposes and methods of this preliminary stage of study. Do not get bogged down in any details along the course of your quick reading. Read more for overall impressions, trying to sense the atmosphere of Moses' message. Record a title for each chapter of the book on the following chart. (Note that our outline begins a segment at 4:44 instead of at 5:1. Why should there be an alteration in the location of this division?)

B. Survey Outline.

There are two major tasks to be accomplished in this phase

---

*G. T. Manley, ed., *New Bible Handbook*, (Chicago: Inter-Varsity Press, 1950), p. 147.

†*Gleason L. Archer, A Survey of Old Testament Introduction*, (Chicago: Moody Press, 1964), p. 244.

of Bible study: (1) to identify the *principal* truth of the book as a whole; and (2) to find how the parts of the book gather under *groups,* each group related to the whole.

1. *Principal truth.* Something has already been said about this in the section entitled *Setting.* Arrive at your own conclusions as to what this principal truth is. Write out the theme of Deuteronomy in your own words. Do as much work on this as you can before reading any further in this lesson.

Deuteronomy can be called one long, varied plea for hearty obedience to God, based on the two grand motives of love and fear.

This plea for obedience is long, and Moses varied it in every way, shape and manner. He pled not only for obedience but for *hearty* obedience, basing the plea on the people's love for God and fear of Him. God had given Moses the ability to see far down the ages by lifting the veil which hides the future from mortal eyes. Moses saw the path of obedience stretching out to the right and he saw the path of disobedience stretching to the left. He saw what would be the consequences to the nation if they took the path of obedience. Their future would be so glorious that words could scarcely depict it. He also saw what would be the consequences to the nation if they took the path of disobedience. Their future would be so dark and dreadful that he would prefer to cast it from his mind.

Moses faithfully set both these paths before the nation, with a mighty appeal to take the one to the right. It seems that Moses in this farewell address exhausted all his resources in the way of persuasion. His one grand object was to move the people to obedience. As he argued from their past history, their present blessed condition and what God had shown him of their future, it was as though, in his great yearning over them, he would lift the whole nation in his arms up to the high spiritual plateau where he himself was living.

One title that has been assigned Deuteronomy is The Book of Remembrance. This is an appropriate title, for not only is one entire section devoted to the command "remember" (1:1—4:43), but the command reappears throughout the book. Read 4:9, 23; 5:15; 6:12; 8:2, 11, 18;

DEUTERONOMY THE BOOK OF REMEMBRANCE

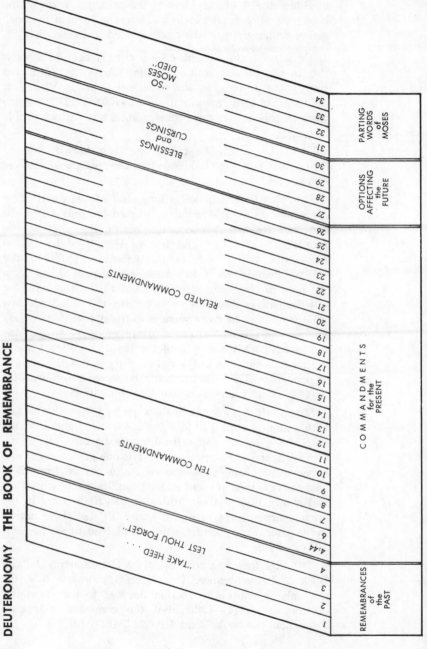

REMEMBRANCES of the PAST	COMMANDMENTS for the PRESENT		OPTIONS AFFECTING the FUTURE	PARTING WORDS of MOSES

"TAKE HEED . . . LEST THOU FORGET"

TEN COMMANDMENTS

RELATED COMMANDMENTS

BLESSINGS and CURSINGS

"SO MOSES DIED"

4:44

9:7; 24:9; 25:17. Of these verses, 4:23 and 8:11 might be considered key verses.

2. *Groups.* Our purpose here is to identify groups of chapters in Deuteronomy, depending on similar content. Try to locate such groups on your own, before proceeding to study the following outline.

The first division, 1:1—4:43, reviews Israel's journeys from Egypt to Moab.

Observe from the chart that the largest division of Deuteronomy records the commandments of God for the day-by-day living of the Israelites. Then beginning at chapter 27 Moses says very emphatically that there are only two options set before the Israelites and that their future (blessing or curse) depends on which choice they make. The last section (chaps. 31-34) records Moses' parting words and the record of his death and burial. There could be no more appropriate ending to the book of Deuteronomy and to the Pentateuch as well.

"And there arose not a prophet since in Israel like unto Moses . . ." (34:10).

As a fitting conclusion to this lesson's study, read 1:1-8 and 34:1-8 in sequence. As great a man as Moses was, the exalted Person of Deuteronomy is the Lord Himself. Your reading of these verses will bear this out.

Remembrances of the Past

THESE FOUR CHAPTERS WERE INTENDED

TO FOCUS THE ISRAELITES' EYES ON THE PAST,

WITH THE VIEW TO FUTURE BLESSING.

The words were spoken by Moses to the people encamped on the plains of Moab just before they broke camp to cross the Jordan into Canaan (1:1-5).

I. ANALYSIS.

The approaches of studying this section of Deuteronomy are innumerable and challenging! The suggestions offered will start you on paths of study; it is up to you to pursue the courses to the end and to launch out on new courses on your own. Keep one prominent question before you at all times: What was Moses trying to teach the Israelites in each thing he said?

Read through the chapters once or twice, making special note of key words and clauses. Observe also in this reading any turning points in subject matter. On the following chart record paragraph titles for each paragraph shown. This exercise should give you a fair acquaintance with the flow of the narrative.

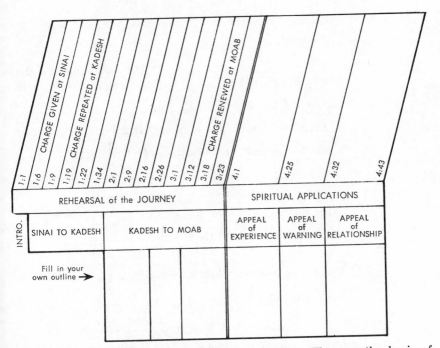

Study the outlines shown above. Then on the basis of your own study expand on the outlines in the spaces shown.

After you have completed the above, you will be ready to analyze each segment individually. The following study suggestions touch on some of the more important parts of this passage. They will serve as starters for study; your own analysis should reach all parts of the various segments.

1. Note the places where the charge "Go in and possess the land" appears. Study the different contexts of the command, and the truths associated with it.

2. Read 1:9-18. Why did Moses remind the people of the helpers he had been given? _____

3. Read 1:22-46. Why would Moses have been pleased (v. 23) with the people's suggestion of reconnaissance? _____

What did Moses mean by the words "for your sakes" in verse 37? _____

_____ In what sense did the the Israelite children have "no knowledge between good and evil"? (v. 39). _____

4. Chapter 2. How do you know that 2:1 is *after* the long wilderness period? (read further into the chapter). _____

_____ What is the impact of verse 25?

_____

What do you learn from this chapter about God's hand in the history of nations? Be specific. _____

_____

What should be the Christian outlook on current events in the world today? _____

_____

5. Compare the geography of 3:12-17 with that of 3:18-22.

6. What was the lesson concerning the two kings in 3:21?

_____

7. Compare the contexts of "I commanded you" (3:18) and "I besought the LORD" (3:23). Why did Moses recall the experience of 3:23-26? _____

_____ What different purposes were behind God's reply (3:26-29)? _____

_____

8. Read 4:1-43. Compare verses 3 and 9. What is the content of verses 10-14? _____

Which was more important for the Israelites: the experiences or the words? _____

Contrast the "I" and the "ye" of verse 22.

Compare the contexts of "forget" in verses 23 and 31.
What motivation was Moses appealing to in verses 32-40?

II. COMMENTS.

The words of Moses recorded in Deuteronomy were delivered to Israel as a reaffirmation of the covenant relationship between God and His people. The pattern followed by Moses in delivering his message has been compared with the approach used by kings of Moses' day in addressing their subjects. Meredith Kline writes of this: "Part of the standard procedure followed in the ancient Near East when great kings thus gave covenants to vassal peoples was the preparation of a text of the ceremony as the treaty document and witness. The book of Deuteronomy is the document prepared by Moses as a witness to the dynastic covenant which the Lord gave to Israel in the plains of Moab (cf. 31:26)."*

It was natural for Moses to refer to history first and let experience be a teacher. Not every event in Israel's journey from Egypt was reviewed, but only those from which Moses would draw his arguments. In substance, what he said was:

"You see how it has been for the past forty years. Whenever this nation obeyed God it has been blessed, and whenever it has disobeyed Him it has been punished; therefore in the future obey."

Observe from verses 2 and 3 of the first chapter how much time Israel lost by disobedience:

"There are eleven days journey from Horeb by the way of Mount Seir unto Kadesh-barnea. And it came to pass in the fortieth year . . . ."

Forty years to make an eleven-day journey! Someone has remarked, "They were slow travelers because they were slow learners." Some of us are slow travelers in the spiritual life for the same reason.

Before moving on to the next lesson, be sure to write out a list of the timeless universal truths the passage teaches. It will amaze you how contemporary such an ancient book can be.

---

*C. F. Pfeiffer and E. F. Harrison (eds.), *The Wycliffe Bible Commentary* (Chicago: Moody Press, 1962), p. 155.

III. SUMMARY.

In this passage Moses shows the intimate relationship of Israel's history (past, present, future) to the word and covenant of Israel's God. This may be diagramed as follows:

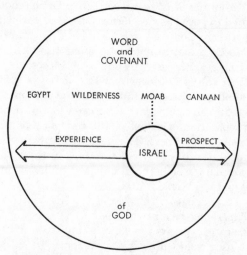

Observe that the small circle (Israel) is contained within the large circle (Word and Covenant of God). As a summary exercise, show how the relationships shown by the diagram are illustrated in the first four chapters of Deuteronomy.

Commandments
for the Present

BECAUSE SO MANY CHAPTERS ARE INVOLVED

IN THIS LESSON, YOU MAY WANT

TO STUDY THE PASSAGE IN SMALLER UNITS.

With this in mind, this lesson has been divided into two units, each of which may be studied as a separate lesson.

These chapters of Deuteronomy comprise the largest section of the book. Moses had just finished rehearsing the experiences of Israel since the day they left Egypt. Toward the end of that rehearsal he reminded the people of the great event at Sinai when the Maker of heaven and earth talked to them from the fiery, smoking, quaking mountain. Said Moses, "Ask now of the days that are past, which were before thee, since the day that God created man upon the earth, and ask from the one side of heaven unto the other, whether there hath been any such thing as this great thing is, or hath been heard like it? Did ever people hear the voice of God speaking out of the midst of the fire, as thou hast heard, and live?" (4:32-33).

How could Israel ever forget that day? And to guard against any idea that this law had been given only to their fathers, and was therefore out-of-date and not binding upon this new generation, Moses reminded the people:

"The LORD made not this covenant with our fathers, but with us, even us, who are all of us here alive this day" (5:3).

Now it was Moses' task to declare again the law which God had originally given, and to add to it other testimonies, statutes and judgments. These were God's commandments for Israel's day-by-day living, commandments for their ever-present today.

Unit One: The Ten Commandments (4:44—11:32)

I. ANALYSIS.

These chapters concern primarily the ten commandments, and of the ten the first commandment is given preeminence.

The organization of these chapters is not too easily detected. The following suggestions for analysis and synthesis are intended to help you see *groups* of subjects treated by Moses.

First, read through the chapters once to catch the feeling of the section and to note the highlights. Now return to each smaller part with a view to closer scrutiny.

Read each paragraph shown below (in some instances a few paragraphs are grouped together). Write out a sentence for each paragraph stating the main content of the paragraph. In some instances you may choose to quote a key verse instead. (Note: Only the reference of the first verse of each paragraph is given below.)

Use the two outlines shown at the right of the table (Israel; God) to help you relate each paragraph to a common theme.

After you have completed this exercise, study further into your own identifications of main content, and try to work out your own outline.

Observe how the last section (10:12—11:32) returns to similar thoughts of the earlier section 4:44—6:25.

For a practical exercise, write a list of at least ten key verses (or parts of verses) that teach important truths applicable to Christian living today.

What do you consider to be the three most prominent lessons of these chapters?

PARAGRAPH	MAIN CONTENT	ISRAEL	GOD
4:44			
5:6			
5:22		ENLIGHTENED PEOPLE	GOD SPEAKS
6:1			
6:4			
6:20			
7:1			
7:6		SPECIAL PEOPLE	GOD EMPOWERS
7:12			
7:17			
8:1		DEPENDENT PEOPLE	GOD PROVIDES
8:11			
9:1			
9:7		STIFF-NECKED PEOPLE	GOD IS GRACIOUS
10:1			
10:12			
11:1		ACCOUNTABLE PEOPLE	GOD IS JUST
11:8			
11:26			

II. COMMENTS.

Observe that Moses in this review of the law (4:44—26:19) first briefly rehearsed the general principles of the law as contained in the Ten Commandments. Throughout the rest of the section he not only reviewed the law more at length but he also made comments on it. Because of the limitation of space this study guide cannot dwell upon all the priceless spiritual and practical lessons contained in these inspired chapters. Attention will be called to some of the important things, but it is recommended that every part of the book receive careful, prayerful meditation. Those who do this will be richly repaid.

Mark especially what God says about the importance of the Israelites keeping the law of God before them (6:6-9), because the same words can be applied to your own personal relationship to the Bible. Read these verses slowly and thoughtfully, and examine your own life by them. Is God's Word in your heart or is it only in your head? Are you teaching God's Word diligently to your children? Do you talk of what God has said when you are sitting at home or walking along the street? Do you speak of His Word on retiring for the night and on rising in the morning?

God knew the heart of His people. He knew they would be surrounded by tribes and nations who worshiped all kinds of idols. Unless they kept His worship and statutes prominently before them, they would become interested in other things and forget Him. The human heart is ever the same. Unless we keep God's work and God's Word continually before us, it is very easy to become interested in other work and other things and to forget Him. We cannot but be impressed with the kindness and condescension of God in explaining why all these commands are to be obeyed (for example, 7:3-4, 6-8). Verse 6 of chapter 7 should be sufficient motive for every child of God to keep himself from the things of sin and to seek to live according to his high calling in Christ.

In Deuteronomy 8:10-20 God warned the people that when they had received the fertile land of Canaan from the Lord and when they had prospered by His blessing, they must not take the credit to themselves nor consider themselves self-made men, saying, "my power and the might of mine hand hath gotten me this wealth." They were to remember that the Lord their God had given them power to get the wealth. Moreover, they were not to suppose that when they fought with and conquered their enemies in Canaan that God had given them the victory because of any merit of their own. It would be because the nations were so evil, not because Israel had such a good record, that the Lord would drive out the inhabitants (9:4-6). To impress this upon them, Moses reviewed some of their rebellions and disobedience (9:7-24).

We, as well as Israel, need this warning against pride.

Sometimes we are tempted to congratulate ourselves and suppose that we deserve all credit when God has graciously given us the victory over spiritual enemies, some besetting sin or great temptation, or when He has blessed us with temporal or spiritual riches. When we feel like that, it would be well to look back over our life and to acknowledge those times of our rebellion, failure and disobedience, and to cry out, as Jacob did, "I am not worthy of the least of all the mercies, and of all the truth, which thou hast shewed unto thy servant" (Gen. 32:10).

Unit Two: Related Commandments (12:1—26:9)

In the previous chapters (4:44—11:32) emphasis was put on *who God is* and *what He basically demands*. In the chapters of this second unit, two of the more prominent items are the *place of worship* ("the place which the LORD your God shall choose," 12:5, 11), and the people's new *homeland*. Thus much is written in these chapters about true worship and laws for everyday living. The commandments here are basically the Ten Commandments amplified and specified. As you study this section always keep in mind the context of the previous chapters.

First, read through the entire section paragraph by paragraph, according to the paragraph divisions in your Bible (in some Bibles, paragraph divisions are indicated by asterisks). Be sure you know the main point of each paragraph. Record this with a word or two in the margin of your Bible.

In this reading you should also be alert to:

a. prominent paragraphs

b. key words and phrases (observe, for example, every occurrence of "the place which the LORD your God shall choose"

c. large movements of thought

d. grouping of paragraphs of similar content

e. general atmosphere

In order to help you see some of the organization of content in this section of Deuteronomy, an outline is given identifying segments and grouping of segments. You may want to follow this outline as you read the passage, or you may choose to refer to it after you have read the chapters.

DEUTERONOMY 12:1—26:19

SEGMENT	MAIN CONTENT	THEME	RIGHTEOUSNESS
12:1ff.		WARNINGS of IDOLATRY	
13:1			
14:1			CEREMONIAL RIGHTEOUSNESS
22		LAWS of WORSHIP and LIVING	
15:1			
19			
16:18		QUALIFICATIONS of LEADERS	
19:1		PRINCIPLES of PEACE AND WAR	GOVERNMENTAL RIGHTEOUSNESS
20:1			
21:15		LAWS of LIVING	PRACTICAL RIGHTEOUSNESS
"When thou art come in unto the land' 26:1			
26:1		ASCRIPTIONS of PRAISE	
26:16		CONCLUSION	

As in the outline given for unit one, a space is left blank opposite each segment. Record in this space the common subject of each segment.

1. See 12:1—13:8. Observe the various contexts where this statement appears: "the place which the LORD your God shall choose." (Continue this study when you analyze the segments that follow.) What place is referred to by this

statement? _____

Why one central place? _____

2. Why is *utter* destruction commanded in 12:2-3? _____

_____Why are such stern measures to be taken against the groups mentioned in

chapter 13? _____

3. See 14:1—16:17. How is 14:2 an introductory verse to

this section? _____

What is the timeless universal principle of 15:1-18? _____

_____

_____What is the

Christian's obligation to his fellowman? _____

_____ What priority did Jesus give to the commandment to love one another?

(Read Matt. 22:35-40). _____

_____

4. See 16:18—18:22. What leaders are referred to in this

section? _____

_____List some of their

qualifications and duties of office. _____

_____

Read Acts 3:22 and 7:37 in connection with Deuteronomy 18:15-19.

5. See 19:1—21:14. List some important spiritual lessons to be learned from this section. What do the chapters teach about God's view of war?

6. See 21:15—25:19. This section contains many laws for the Israelites' living. What can be learned from them for Christian living today? In answering this question, try to identify the timeless, universal principle behind the laws under consideration.

7. See 26:1-15. Consider the appropriateness of the location of this segment at the end of this long section of Deuteronomy.

8. See 26:16-19. Analyze this paragraph closely. Take special note of this twin:

"Thou hast avouched [declared] the LORD this day . . ."

"And the LORD hath avouched [declared] thee this day . . ."

II. COMMENTS.

A. False Teachers.

From Deuteronomy 13 we learn how grave an offense it was for a person to persuade others to turn away from the worship of God and the keeping of His commandments. So great was the sin that such a person was to be put to death immediately and the one to whom the suggestion was made was to be the first to stone the offender, even if the offender were of closest kin (see vv. 6-10). The offender was to be treated as a murderer, as one who sought the death of a soul. God's opinions about the gravity of such a sin have not changed, as can be seen by Mark 9:42, and those who are seeking to undermine the faith of believers in Christ and the Bible would do well to take heed.

B. Righteous Leaders.

The remarkable prophetic insight of Moses into the future history of Israel is illustrated in chapter 17, where Moses anticipates that they will ask God to give them a king. Compare verse 14 with I Samuel 8:5, 19-20 and notice that Moses tells them the very words which will be used when the people shall request a king. They said they wanted a king "like all the nations." "Like all the nations" is exactly what God did not want them to be. He wanted them to be a separate, distinct and peculiar people, as He wants Christians to be today.

Other nations were to copy them; they were not to copy other nations. But we see in I Samuel 8 that they grew tired of God's way, and preferred the ways of the surrounding nations. They were determined to be in fashion at any cost! It is better for God's people to be out of fashion according to the world than to be out of favor with God.

Note the four things forbidden of any future king:

"He shall not multiply horses to himself, nor cause the people to return to Egypt, to the end that he should multiply horses. . . . Neither shall he multiply wives to himself, that his heart turn not away: neither shall he greatly multiply to himself silver and gold" (17:16-17).

Now turn to I Kings 10 and 11, observing that four hundred and fifty years later these forbidden things were done by Solomon, the very wisest king that Israel ever had (see I Kings 10:26-28; 11:3-4)! How can we explain that Israel's wisest king did the four things which a king was expressly forbidden to do? We do not have to look far into Deuteronomy 17 to find the reason. Only kings who lived and ruled by God's Book would keep from evil:

"And it shall be, when he sitteth upon the throne of his kingdom, that he shall write him a copy of this law in a book out of that which is before the priests the Levites: and it shall be with him, and he shall read therein all the days of his life; that he may learn to fear the LORD his God, to keep all the words of this law and these statutes, to do them" (17:18-19). Someone has commented of Solomon that "the cause of all the wreck and ruin that so rapidly followed the splendor of Solomon's reign was *neglect of the plain Word of God.*" This is fair warning to Christian leaders and laymen today.

C. Faithful Stewardship.

In Deuteronomy 18:1-8 Moses reminded the people that the Levites who were chosen of God to minister continually about the tabernacle were given no inheritance of land. Therefore the people must be careful to see that the Levites were supported by gifts and offerings made unto the Lord.

All through Israel's history, a healthful spiritual condition meant that the altar of God was well attended and God's ministers—the priests and Levites—were consequently well supplied. But when spirituality was at a low ebb in Israel, the people were not faithful in their gifts to God and consequently the priests and Levites had little or no support.

This same principle of stewardship applies to the support of the Christian ministry. See Paul's remarks on the subject in I Corinthians 9:6-11. No one in Israel could put himself into the office of priest or Levite and claim support of the tribes. Only those whom the Lord Himself had called and appointed could minister thus. Moreover, even these ministers were not to demand anything of the people, as did Eli's wicked sons, or even so much as look to the people for their support. They were to look to God alone, as Moses often said, "The LORD is their inheritance" (18:2). Nor were the people to give to the Levites merely with a view to their support. They were to bring their offerings "unto the LORD," and present them to Him. The spirit in which the Levites were to do their work is the spirit in which all work for the Lord should be done:

"And if a Levite come from any of thy gates . . . and come with all the desire of his mind unto the place which the LORD shall choose; then he shall minister in the name of the LORD his God, as all his brethren the Levites do, which stand there before the LORD" (18:6-7).

D. Sources of Revelation.

In 18:9-22 Moses identifies two contrasting sources of revelation—the false (vv. 9-14, 20) and the true (vv. 15-22).

Moses warned the Israelites against having anything to do with any of these occult practices of the inhabitants of Canaan: divination, soothsaying, observing omens, sorcery, consulting familiar spirits and necromancy. Such evil practices would cause God to drive the people out of the land.

These abominations are identical in spirit with today's fortune-telling, clairvoyance, mesmerism and especially all forms of spiritualism. God hates them all and plainly warns His people against them. This warning is seen to be timely, and wisely applicable to the church, when one observes that even professing Christians are in the habit of consulting fortune-tellers, witnessing magical occultism and participating in table tilting and spirit rapping. One has wisely questioned, "What do those who hold in their hands a perfect revelation from God want with table turning and spirit rapping?" Isaiah's answer is, "Should not a people seek unto their God? . . . To the law and to the testimony" (Isa. 8:19-20). A Christian should go to God and God's Word to learn about himself, the future and the way he should take. How absurd for a Christian who has bold access to the throne of God to seek to call up the dead or to consult with spirits for direction.

In contrast to all this, Moses pointed the Israelites to the Prophet whom the Lord God would raise up (see Deut. 18:15). This Prophet was Jesus Christ, as seen by Peter's application of Moses' words (Acts 3:22-23), although its *immediate* reference was probably to Joshua. When Christ's blessed voice can be heard, why listen to the voice of a wizard or that of a consulter with familiar spirits who can only "peep and . . . mutter" (Isa. 8:19)?*

E. Peace and War.

In chapter 20 God instructs Israel about warfare. We have earlier dwelt upon the wisdom and justice of God in destroying the wicked and rebellious Canaanites, using Israel as His instrument in executing judgment. One should have no difficulty in reconciling the type of command contained in verses 16-18 with the benevolent character of God.

Israel was to fight the Lord's battles, and these two qualifications were necessary for such a conflict: first, a bold, clear confidence in God; and second, a heart entirely disentangled from the things of nature and of earth. Concerning the latter, the mere possession of a house, vineyard or wife did not disqualify a man for the Lord's battles. These were not hindrances unless possessing them involved entanglement so that his heart and his mind would be engaged with *them* rather than with the conflict on hand.

Christians are called to carry on a constant spiritual warfare. The same qualifications are demanded of the soldier who would engage in this fight against principalities, against powers, against world rulers of this darkness, against wicked spirits in the heavenlies. What the Canaan-

---

*A book which is very helpful in studying this subject is: Merrill F. Unger, *Biblical Demonology* (Wheaton, Ill.: Scripture Press, 1952).

ites were to the Israelites, the wicked spirits in the heavenlies are to us.

F. Laws of Living.

In the sundry laws of living contained in 21:15—25:19 there was one grand fact that the people were to keep ever before them. It was that the Lord God was present in their midst. That was sufficient reason for all the care regarding purity, justice and righteousness. The fact of God's presence in the camp was to "govern their most private habits and give character to all their ways." "For the LORD thy God walketh in the midst of thy camp . . . *therefore* shall thy camp be holy" (Deut. 23:14).

✳   ✳   ✳   ✳

III. SUMMARY.

The paragraph 26:16-19 is an appropriate summary of the chapters of this lesson. Reviewing some of the subjects contained in those chapters, parts of verses 16 and 19 might be amplified to read like this:

"This day the LORD THY GOD
hath commanded THEE—
enlightened people
special people
dependent people
stiff-necked people
accountable people—
to do these STATUTES AND JUDGMENTS
for—
ceremonial righteousness
governmental righteousness
practical righteousness . . .
that He might make thee
high above all nations which he hath made . . .
that thou mayest be
a holy people unto the LORD THY GOD."

Options
Determining the Future

MOSES COMES NOW TO THAT POINT

     IN HIS DISCOURSE WHEN HE STORMS

THE WILL OF THE HEARERS,

offering them only two options—either hearken or reject—
to determine their future destiny—either life or death.

As you study this passage reflect on the awesome truth
that the either-or challenge to souls is the same today as
it was in Moses' day. It will not surprise you how contemporary these chapters are in their spiritual application.

I. ANALYSIS.

As you read these chapters in one sitting, decide on a paragraph title for each of the thirteen paragraphs shown on the
following chart (note that 28:25-68 is treated as only one
paragraph; look for the *common* subject). Record your
own titles on a chart of your own. Continue in this obser-
vation stage of study, following suggestions of previous
lessons.

Next, study the outline shown below, seeking to understand why groups of paragraphs are identified as they are.
Refer to the biblical text whenever necessary.

1. References to *time* are keys to an understanding of this
passage. Observe for example that 27:2 refers to the ap-
proaching day of crossing the Jordan; the section 28:25ff.
describes future captivity to a foreign nation if the people

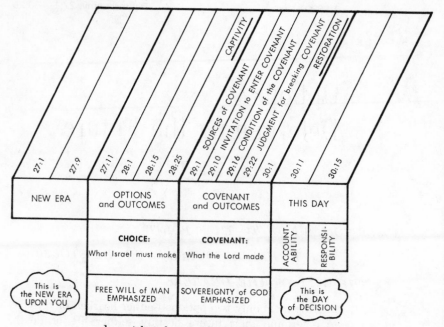

do not hearken to God; and 30:1-3 prophesies a future return from captivity.

2. Read 27:1-10. What is the relation between the stones for the law and stones for the altar? _____

_____

What is the significance of the time reference in verse 9*b:* "This day thou art become the people of the LORD thy God"? _____

3. Read 27:11-13. Why the drama of the ceremony associated with Mounts Ebal and Gerizim? _____

_____

4. Read 28:25-68. Notice all the references to captivity and the captor (nation from afar). Observe from the context how accurately the Assyrian and Babylonian captivities of a later day answered to these descriptions (cf. II Kings 24:18ff. and II Chron. 36:17ff.).

5. Read 29:1—30:10. Observe the frequency of the word "covenant." Note what things are said about the covenant here. Who makes the covenant?_____

_____Observe how the sovereignty of God is emphasized in this word. Compare this with the emphasis of free will of man in the choices of 27: 11—28:68.

6. Read 30:11-14. What tremendous truth is asserted in this paragraph? _____

7. Read 30:15-20. What are some of the incentives given here to promote the right choice? _____

_____

8. List ten vital lessons you have learned from this section of Deuteronomy.

II. COMMENTS.

One of the first things Israel was to do on establishing themselves in the land of Canaan was to march to Mount Ebal and Mount Gerizim, two mountains in the center of the country (locate on a map), and there set up great plastered stones on which the law of God was to be written. Six tribes were to stand upon Mount Gerizim to declare blessing upon the people for obedience to this law, and the other six tribes were to stand upon Mount Ebal to declare curses upon the people for disobedience.

The consequences of obeying this law as well as the consequences of disobeying it are set forth in chapter 28. The first fourteen verses give a bright picture of the nation's future if they will take the path of obedience. From these verses we learn how blessed, rich and powerful Israel could have been if they had been true to God. The nation would have been invincible (v. 10) and might indeed have become the head and not the tail among all the nations of the earth.

The tone changes at verse 15 and from there onward we have a picture of the black future awaiting the nation if they should take the path of disobedience. Observe how the punishments foretold in these verses grow more and more severe with each verse. The punishments are conditional in the context of prophecy, and history has confirmed the accuracy of the prophecies with respect to the Jewish nation. Note these prophecies and their fulfillment concerning the Jews.*

1. They would be so sorely besieged by enemies that women would devour their own children.

—Fulfilled in the sieges of Jerusalem both under Nebuchadnezzar and under Titus.

2. They would be rooted out of their land and carried afar into captivity.

—Fulfilled in the Babylonian and Assyrian captivities.

3. They were not to find rest in any of the lands of their captivity, but would be scattered abroad and driven hither and thither as wanderers among all nations.

—Fulfilled in the past and being fulfilled in the present.

4. They would be despoiled by their enemies and made a prey.

—Fulfilled in every land where they have dwelt; and if, as in Great Britain and the United States, they have been treated with more consideration, it is owing to the permeating influence of the Christian religion.

5. They would be a "byword," an "astonishment," a "hissing" in the nations where they were scattered.

—They have been compelled in some cases even to wear a distinctive badge and occupy what has been invidiously known as the "Jewish quarter."

6. While scattered among all nations they would still be separate.

—It is a strange historic phenomenon that this race has never incorporated in or amalgamated with the nations among whom they have dwelt. When Irishmen, Scotsmen, Germans and Italians come to America, in the course of a few generations they become integral parts of one homogeneous American people. But the Jew still remains a Jew, except when by becoming a Christian he ceases to be distinctively a Jew and identifies himself with Christian fellowships.

---

*Taken from A. T. Pierson, *God's Living Oracles* (N. Y.: The Baker & Taylor Co., 1904).

7. They would ultimately be restored to their own land, grafted back into their own olive tree, and the covenant privileges which had been suspended during the times of the Gentiles would be restored to them.

—This remains to be fulfilled.

Anyone who is skeptical about the inspiration of the words of Scripture should consider whether it is possible that such a complex historical phenomenon as this would or could have been clearly foretold by Moses, without divine foresight, in one of the most ancient books of the human race. Surely the foreknowledge of such facts must have been communicated by the omniscient God. It is said that when one of the great monarchs of Europe asked his chaplain to give him in a word an evidence that the Bible was from God, the answer was "the Jew."

Note the last of the seven prophecies mentioned above and read carefully Deuteronomy 30:1-6. It is as though Moses saw this ray of hope which is the promise of restoration for this people so beloved of God, gleaming in the distance beyond all the curses just enumerated. In the light of such promises to Israel and especially in the light of Deuteronomy 30:7, should not the Gentiles more earnestly and sincerely pray for the Jew? See the blessing promised in Psalm 122:6 for those who do.

Moses closed his farewell address to the people with a mighty appeal for obedience (read 30:15-20). As shown in the book of Joshua, they did walk in this path of obedience for a little while. But they rebelled against God again and again, and all the threatened curses have been poured out upon them. To this day they suffer under the heavy judgment.

III. CONCLUSION.

Moses did his best for Israel. He led them from the bondage of Egypt and for forty years he bore their murmurings and backslidings and rebellion; and with his latest breath he pled with them for their own good to obey their God. "I call heaven and earth to record this day against you that I have set before you life and death, blessing and cursing; therefore choose life that both thou and thy seed may live" (30:19).

Parting Words of Moses

THE PEOPLE WHO HAVE BEEN CAMPING ON THE
EAST SIDE OF THE JORDAN, WAITING TO CROSS OVER,
ARE GIVEN THEIR FINAL CHARGES,

a summary interpretation of the philosophy of God's judgments in history and a reminder of the blessings awaiting
the people in the land. To make the book complete God
inspired a writer to attach to Moses' writings a record of
the fact of Moses' death. (Read again 1:1-8 before con-
tinuing your study.)

I. ANALYSIS AND COMMENTS.

These chapters are unusually interesting, partly because
of the atmosphere of expectation. Read through the chapters carefully, then do the steps of study.

The following outline shows the *main* content of each
of the four chapters.

31:1 CHARGE	31:30 SONG	33:1 BENEDICTION	34:1 DEPARTURE
CHALLENGE to DEVOTION	WITNESS of GOD'S JUDGMENTS	BLESSINGS on ISRAEL	CHANGE of LEADERSHIP
W O R D			EVENT

Paragraphical study of these chapters is an excellent approach to use. Following the paragraph divisions in the accompanying chart, record a brief identification of the main content of each paragraph in the spaces provided (see examples).

A. Charge (31:1-29).

PARAGRAPH	MAIN CONTENT
31:1-6	Moses' charge to Israel
31:7-8	Moses' charge to Joshua
31:9-13	
31:14-23	
31:24-29	

What are the prominent things said in each charge?

_____

_____

_____Is there anything

common to all of them? _____

_____

Comments: Basically, the charge to the people and their leaders was, "The Lord is with you; fear not." Obviously fear was one of the people's enemies. Across the Jordan they would face seven strong nations who had been entrenched in great walled cities for hundreds of years. These fierce Canaanites were well versed in warfare; and humanly speaking, this young, inexperienced nation of Israel would be no match.

Moses, their great leader, was about to leave them, and Joshua, the new leader, was comparatively untried. So it is no wonder that their courage began to ebb. But what stirring words Moses used to encourage the people (vv. 3-6). He pointed them far above and beyond Joshua to their true Leader, God. It mattered little what human leader stood before them when their great God who had been leading them was still at their head. His charge must have been particularly strengthening to Joshua, who no doubt realized the heavy responsibilities which were being laid upon him and was feeling keenly being left alone without Moses. And Moses was especially speaking to Joshua when he said the words of verses 7-8: "And the LORD, he it is that doth go before thee; he will be with thee, he will not fail thee, neither forsake thee: fear not, neither be dismayed."

This is what confronts Christians today: strong and fierce enemies, hard and bitter battles, the loss of those upon whom we have leaned most heavily for comfort and advice, loneliness and discouragement. But these precious words which have been ringing down the ages should touch our hearts and stir us to fresh courage and resolve, as we realize that they are just as true for us as they were for Israel:

"Be strong and of a good courage, fear not, nor be afraid of them: for the LORD thy God, he it is that doth go with thee; he will not fail thee, nor forsake thee."

How touching and beautiful it is to see Moses, the white-haired, faithful old servant of God, standing there among the people, the only one of the company who could not enter Canaan. Perceive his sweet submission to God's will—not a word of murmuring, not the least reproach, not the slightest envy or jealousy of the one who should take his place. Even though he had to be left behind, Moses did not think of himself; his great thought was to encourage others to press forward.

Deuteronomy is full of Moses' oft-repeated exhortation and insistence upon familiarity with God's Word. It is the great burden of the book from beginning to end. In addition to the daily home reading, teaching and speaking of God's Word, we have the command that at the end of every seven years all Israel should be gathered together at a central meeting place which God should appoint. At that time the law was to be publicly read so that all the people—men, women and children—might be acquainted with its teaching.

B. Song (31:30—32:52).

PARAGRAPH	MAIN CONTENT
31:30	Title
32:1-3	Invocation
32:4-6	
32:7-25	
32:26-42	
32:43-47	
32:48-52	

Notice the purpose of the song: 31:19.
How would the words of the song fulfill that purpose?

_____

Divide the paragraph 32:7-25 into these three smaller
paragraphs, and identify contents: 7:14; 15-18; 19-25.
What is taught in verses 26-42 about God's ways in his-

tory? _____

_____

What does this contribute to a Christian view of history?

_____

_____

Comments: Before Moses died he was instructed of God to
compose a song and teach it to the Israelites in order that
they might always remember the reasons for God's judgments. Sometimes the words of a song linger longer in the
memory than do the words of a sermon. God left nothing
undone to fortify Israel at every point against turning unto
other gods.

Observe the audience to which these words were ad-
dressed (v. 1): "Give ear, O ye heavens, and I will speak;
and hear, O earth, the words of my mouth."

Heaven and earth were to listen to the account of God's
dealings with His people and their behavior toward Him.
Surely it would be as God had told Moses—a witness
against them. This song presents God's dealings with Israel
from first to last as well as their sin and the divine wrath

and judgment which follow. See how it maps out their history as Moses has already rehearsed it in chapter 28. First God's goodness is set forth (vv. 7-14); then their idolatrous wickedness (vv. 15-18); next their punishment (vv. 19-25); God's reasons for not utterly destroying them (vv. 26-33); and their redemption at last (vv. 34-43).

How sweetly God's tender care for His people is described (vv. 9-14). How fitly is the Lord shown to be the Rock, that firm unchanging Foundation of everything. And how plainly He teaches that although He will use the nations of the earth as His rod to punish Israel, yet if these nations go beyond what He appoints them "He will break the rod in pieces" and make it manifest to all that He Himself is dealing with His beloved though erring people for their ultimate blessing and His own glory (vv. 27, 41-43).

C. Benediction (33:1-56).

Study especially the concluding paragraph of 33:26-29. What great truths are taught here?
Comments: While the theme of judgment appeared often in chapter 32, this chapter's theme is blessing. You will recall that when Jacob was about to die he gathered his twelve sons about him and blessed them (Gen. 49). So Moses, a second father to the Israelites, gathered these children of Israel (grown now to twelve strong tribes) about him and blessed them just before his death. During the forty years he had served as their leader, Moses had spoken many words to the people. They were words of instruction, reproof and condemnation, but his last words were words of blessing.

There is a great difference between Jacob's blessing and Moses' blessing. Some people, ever ready to see flaws in God's Word, point to these differences as discrepancies or contradictions. But there can be no contradictions when everything comes from the same divine Source. The differences are not contradictions. Note the following:

Jacob sets forth the history of the behavior of his sons. Moses presents the workings of divine grace in them and toward them.

Jacob views his sons in their personal history. Moses views them in their covenant relationship with Jehovah.

The sad part of the story is that though the blessings

were promised, the people forfeited them by their disobedience to God.

D. Departure (34:1-29).

PARAGRAPH	MAIN CONTENT
34:1-8	
34:9	
34:10-12	

What important truths are taught in verse 9? _____

_____

NO PROPHET LIKE MOSES (10-12): Recall from your
study of the life of Moses why such an epitaph could be
written over his grave.
Comments: This last chapter of Deuteronomy is an "inspired postscript" which gives the account of Moses' death
and burial.

"And Moses went up from the plains of Moab into the
mountain of Nebo to the top of Pisgah." We can almost see
him as he completed his rehearsal of the blessings, turned
from the people and ascended alone to the mountaintop.
How the people would strain their eyes to catch the last
glimpse of his beloved form as it slowly vanished in the distance. Next to God he had been their best friend. People
generally remember vividly and try to carry out the last expressed wishes of loved ones. Perhaps in these last mo-
ments as they saw him passing away from them, the desire
of Moses' great heart was accomplished and the people
unreservedly resolved to surrender to God. In the last part
of verse 9 we read: "And the children of Israel hearkened
unto him [Joshua] and did as the LORD commanded
Moses."

When Moses reached the summit of Pisgah a glorious
sight burst upon his vision: "And the LORD showed him
all the land of Gilead, unto Dan, and all Naphtali, and the
land of Ephraim, and Manasseh, and all the land of Judah,
unto the utmost sea, and the south, and the plain of the val-
ley of Jericho, the city of palm trees, unto Zoar."

With undimmed vision his eye swept this fair inheritance
of God's people. The last thing Moses saw on earth was
this land flowing with milk and honey, this God-chosen

spot which he had so long desired to see but which, because of one hour of unbelief and disobedience, he was not allowed to enter. Dwight L. Moody said that Moses did get into the land of Canaan, but he had to go by way of the throne—referring to the time of the transfiguration of Christ when Moses and Elias talked with Him on the mount.

"And Moses was one hundred and twenty years old when he died; his eye was not dim, nor his natural force abated." He did not die as a feeble, helpless old man, but in the fresh vigor of manhood. It was fitting that Moses should die as strong and vigorous as he had lived. Whenever we think of Moses we think of the law that was given by him. As F. B. Meyer said, "He represents God's holy Law which cannot grow outworn or weak, but always abides in its pristine and perfect strength, though it cannot bring us into God's rest." To Joshua, who typifies Christ, was given the work of bringing the people into God's rest-land.

II. CONCLUSION.

And so Moses died. Another leader stepped upon the scene and from then on all eyes were upon Joshua, a man full of the spirit of wisdom. But the grand old lawgiver was not forgotten. No wonder the people loved him. No wonder they mourned him for thirty days. No wonder they have quoted him as an authority down through the centuries. His was a marvelous life crowded full of rich lessons from first to last. We have studied his life from beginning to end. We have watched him from the cradle to the grave, from the basket of bulrushes to the top of Pisgah, from Egypt to Canaan, from earth to heaven; and we shall one day see him in our Father's home on high.

But great as Moses was, his death did not hinder the onward march of God's people. In the first verse of Joshua we read: "Now after the death of Moses, the servant of the LORD, it came to pass that the LORD spake unto Joshua."

God's work does not cease because a leader dies nor God's utterances cease because a prophet dies. We must not lean too heavily upon any human leader or prophet. All are fallible. All pass away. God's Word and God's works are the important and lasting things.

SUMMARY OF DEUTERONOMY

Standing in view of the land which he was forbidden to enter, Moses gathered the leaders and representatives of his people to his side and stirred up their minds concerning the covenant which God had made with Israel.

PAST. He urged them to remember the past and take heed lest they forget (1:1—4:43).

PRESENT. He pleaded for them to hear the commandments of God and do them, that it might be well with them (4:44—26:19).

FUTURE. He challenged them that he had set before them life and good, and death and evil (27:1—30:20).

And so Moses committed his people, and then his own soul, into the hands of his God whom he knew face to face.

*   *   *

Before you move on to study another book of the Bible, meditate for a time on the ways in which the books of Numbers and Deuteronomy have spoken to your heart. Are you determined to be a more obedient Christian?

NOTES

NOTES

NOTES

Moody Press, a ministry of the Moody Bible Institute, is designed for education, evangelization and edification. If we may assist you in knowing more about Christ and the Christian life, please write us without obligation to: Moody Press, c/o MLM, Chicago, Illinois 60610.